THE
WORD TODAY

ALTON WEDEL

SERMONS FOR THE
SECOND HALF OF PENTECOST

C.S.S. Publishing Company
Lima, Ohio

THE WORD TODAY

Copyright © 1984 by
The C.S.S. Publishing Company, Inc.
Lima, Ohio

All rights reserved. No portion of this book may be reproduced or utilized in any form or by any means, electronic or mechanical including photocopying, without permission in writing from the publisher. Inquiries should be addressed to: The C.S.S. Publishing Company, Inc., 628 South Main Street, Lima, Ohio 45804.

4860/ISBN 0-89536-684-3

TO ERNIE
In His Eighty-Fifth Year
Colleague and Faithful Friend
Child of God
Man in Christ
Life in the Spirit

Table of Contents

Preface

On a sunny spring morning in Saint Louis, more years ago than I care to number, I drove to the beginning of my first graduate course in theology at Concordia Seminary, a study opportunity that had as its title, "The Place of Holy Scripture in Lutheran Theology." It seemed a little strange that after ten years in parish ministry I had enrolled for graduate study and signed on with a choice like this. Certainly I knew the place of Holy Scripture in Lutheran theology! After an exhausting week as pastor of a large Saint Louis area parish, Monday mornings could be spent with greater profit sleeping.

But the next two months, unexpectedly, were to become the single greatest growth period of my life. My debt is to the sainted Dr. Paul Bretscher, our theologian instructor in the course, who then was a member of that faculty that later, even during Dr. Bretscher's dying days, was to be frustrated in service by a movement that sailed under the banner of "purifying."

In particular, it was in the account of the Emmaus disciples, Saint Luke 24, that the treasure of the Old Testament Word, Moses and the prophets, was unearthed for me. The burning-heart experience of the Emmaus disciples became my own experience. The risen Lord walked with them and opened the Scriptures to them, beginning with Moses and the prophets, and "interpreted to them in all the Scriptures the things concerning himself."

In my preaching ministry since then, one year of every three has been a year of preaching the Old Testament Promise, alternating on the three-year cycle with the Gospels and Epistles. The advent of the three-year lectionary cycle provided an assist to that process, and now the coming of the new Common Lectionary offers even greater possibilities in concert with the entire Church. The Promise spoken through the prophets is THE WORD TODAY.

The sermons that follow were prepared to fulfill the request for this publication. Most of the Old Testament texts in the Common Lectionary for the final thirteen Sundays of the Pentecost Season were new in my own personal preaching. They have not stood the test of the *viva vox* in the parish pulpit. But they go forth with the prayer that a good blessing will come to the reader through their use.

My gratitude is here given to Susan Waite, who prepared the manuscript for the publisher with exceptional enthusiasm and commitment, and who, before the material is on the press, will be commissioned with her husband, Robert, to the Central African Republic in the mission of The American Lutheran Church. Susan was also a co-worker and friend during her tenure as coordinator of our parish human services ministry.

Included also is my personal dedication of these efforts to Ernie Clausen, with whom I enjoyed eighteen years as a noble colleague and co-worker. Now in his eighty-fifth year, Ernie came to our parish scene as a lay worker and business manager upon his retirement from a position as lobbyist for the railroad industry in the Congress of the United States. Outside of my own household, no friend has ever been closer to me or provided greater Christian example and inspiration without blemish. The Promise has been his life's foundation all through his years and his heart is aflame with the Holy Spirit. Soli Deo Gloria!

— Alton F. Wedel
Minneapolis

Proper 17 (August 28 — September 3)
Ordinary Time 22
1 Kings 2:1-4, 10-12

The Father Who Wanted His Son To Succeed

Every father who is worthy of the name would like to see his son succeed. From the day the child is born, whether son or daughter, through infancy and childhood and the teenage years, Dad wants to be around to train, to guide, to mold, to love, and to enjoy the child who has been given as a heritage from God. He entertains great hopes and visions for the future, when his child will follow in his footsteps, perhaps pursue the same profession, and succeed him in the family business. If he is very wise he acknowledges the children's freedom to make choices of their own, growing to adulthood in a world quite different from his own with possibilities at hand that he could never dream of. But he will be around to test the choices, counsel, caution, and encourage. He would like to see his son succeed; his daughter too.

There may be times of disappointment, moments of despair and fear when he will ask himself, and often share the question with the children's mother, "Where did I go wrong? Where did I fail?" There may be moments of depression when he realizes that the funds are not sufficient to provide the training or the education needed to fulfill the dreams. And certainly there may be moments of regret when he awakens to the fact that his own pattern or example was at fault. And there may be a child or two, youngsters who overturn their parents' values, claim their inheritance, forsake the faith, and beat a hard path to the pig sty. Frequently, we hear it said that it's a strange, strange world in which to bring up children.

It's a charge from God that takes a heap of loving.

One Last Chance

The Word today is not from Dr. Spock on child psychology or health, but from the Holy Scriptures and a paragraph of history we may be inclined to overlook. It's the story of a father who wanted his son to succeed — in this case, King David, who not only wanted Solomon, his son, to succeed him on the throne of Israel, but to prosper, too, in everything he did, whichever way he turned. This was David's one last chance to pass his heritage along, to stamp his last impression on the kingdom he had ruled for forty years. And this is what he had to say as his last charge to Solomon, "that the Lord may establish his word which he spoke to me," the covenant that he had made with David for a throne that would endure forever.

Parents in this church this morning who have known the heartbreak of a son or daughter on the primrose path, or hell-bent for disaster, whether by their own misparenting or other cause, could talk to David. He would understand. The King had fathered nineteen sons himself, whose names are listed by the Chronicler (1 Chronicles 3:1-8), and others who remain unlisted and are uncounted and unnamed, offspring simply summarized as "sons of concubines." His experience in raising them had been anything but thrilling, and except for infamy, not one of them amounted to a cat scratch in the alleys of Jerusalem.

His first-bort, Amnon, incestuously raped his own half-sister Tamar and was slain in vengeance by half-brother, Absalom.

It was Absalom, the handsome prince with his long flowing hair, who planned the coup that seized the throne from David momentarily until his hair became his own undoing in the branches of an oak tree.

His fourth-born, Adonijah, plotted to secure the throne and had himself anointed king ahead of Solomon in one of the most comic, if not tragic, scenes of Scripture. He was later liquidated, gangland style, as a threat to Solomon.

There was the child born to Bathsheba who had been conceived in his adultery and who, upon his birth, took sick and died, just as the Prophet Nathan had predicted.

And all the rest — Ithream, Elishama, Japhia, and Eliada — who can name them all? The most that can be said for them is that their names have been included in the list of David's progeny.

So David understands the conscience pangs and sense of guilt when parents see the iniquity of the fathers visited upon the children. His own guilt, pain, and fasting as Bathsheba's firstborn burned with fever, can attest to that.

He would understand the grief that sears the soul in tragedy and death, for when it was reported that his young son Absalom had been destroyed and his rebellion ended, David sobbed as he retired to his chamber, "O my son Absalom, my son, my son Absalom. Would I had died instead of you, O Absalom, my son, my son."

And he would understand a father's anger, moving as he had to, even on his death bed, to counteract the schemes of Adonijah's self-will and ambition.

Then there was Solomon, his fourth-born by Bathsheba, and the King's last hope among his sons for one who would succeed him on the throne of Israel. When his time to die drew near, when he was "about to go the way of all the earth," David gave this charge to Solomon: "Be strong, and show yourself a man, and keep the charge of the Lord your God, walking in his ways and keeping his statutes . . . that you may prosper . . . 'There shall not fail you a man on the throne of Israel.'"

Be All That You Can Be

In our own milieu and in our struggle to be stylish, we might read in David's charge to Solomon, "Be strong, and show yourself a man," a father's counsel to be a macho man. But this had been the covenant that God had made with Moses: "I am the Lord your God who brought you out of the land of Egypt, out of the house of bondage. I will be your God, and you will be my people." "This day you have become the people of the Lord your God. You shall therefore obey the voice of the Lord your God, keeping his

commandments and his statutes, which I command you this day."
(Deuteronomy 27:9,10)

David might have said it in the words of the Army commercial
for recruitment: "Be all that you can be," shirking no challenge,
living to your full potential, being faithful to your God and Lord
on every step of life. For a Christian that means living up to what
you are — someone special, a total human being whose core is the
experience of sonship, a partaker in God's total love. To be the
King of Israel was to be the symbol of God's kingly rule among his
people, according to the covenant. To be a child of God is to have
been included in the company of kings and priests who have been
gathered out of every tribe and tongue and nation and presented to
the Lord. "Be all that you can be."

And how did Solomon fare? "Then David slept with his
fathers, and was buried in the city of David . . . So Solomon sat
upon the throne of David his father, and his kingdom was firmly
established." The nation prospered as it never had before.
Diplomacy flourished. The balance of trade was always in the
country's favor. The wisdom of Solomon was heralded around the
world so that even the Queen of Sheba came to test him with hard
questions. (I Kings 10:1) "Solomon in all his glory" became and
still remains a byword through the generations, and the envy of
succeeding kings and emperors and presidents across the centuries
who sought to reach that glory, too. Or can we forget the temple on
Mount Zion, the building and the worship ritual that were his most
magnificent achievements? "Be all that you can be!" — and
Solomon was all that he could be.

But Not Quite All

Not quite, we have to add. The history of succeeding years
reveals that this is not yet what God had in mind when he made
covenant with David for a throne that would endure forever, nor is
this the glory of his kingdom. There is still another Son of David
whom we have not yet mentioned, the One who came without a
shred of glory whatsoever, born in the city of David's lineage and
crucified in the city of David's capital — Great David's greater
Son. What Solomon could never be, he is. What David's highest
hopes could not conceive, the Christ fulfilled. The Son whom
David never saw became the king in whom his kingdom was
established firmly.

The Son of David

Listen for the echoes of this story of succession to the throne of Israel in the life and ministry and death of Jesus Christ. "I am about to go the way of all the earth," King David said, and that's what Jesus said,: "Behold, we are going up to Jerusalem . . . the Son of man will be delivered to the Gentiles . . . and will be mocked and scourged and killed." (St. Luke 18) He went the way of all the earth for us.

"Jesus, Son of David, have mercy on me," screamed the blind man out of his despair, voicing what must be the deepest need of our lives also, not for glory, but for mercy.

Following his coronation at the Gihon spring, the royal ceremony culminated in a great procession through the city streets, Solomon, the Lord's anointed, riding on a mule as people shouted, "Long live King Solomon!" Do you remember it? "Tell the daughter of Zion, Behold, your king is coming to you, humble, mounted on a mule," and those who went before and those who followed after, shouted, "Hosanna to the Son of David! Blessed is he who comes in the name of the Lord!"

This is the Son of David who succeeded, in whom the Lord establishes his word, in whom the kingdom is established forever.

Not by might, but by mercy!

Not a kingdom of this world with fighting armies, but a kingdom of compassion with a worldwide company of servants.

Not a reign of power where all enemies are liquidated, but a reign of grace where we who were his enemies are reconciled to God and death itself is liquidated.

Not an empire where prosperity is measured by the dollar, but a company of Christ's disciples who have laid up treasures in heaven.

David charged his son to follow in the law of Moses, to keep his statutes, his commandments and his testimonies. Jesus Christ who walked that way for us, and who succeeded, now charges us to follow him.

14

Proper 18 (September 4-10)
Ordinary Time 23
Proverbs 2:1-8

The Word To The Wise

Decisions! Decisions! Decisions! Life seems to be one long succession of decisions —

• some of them of small significance that could go either way without upsetting anything;

• others of a knotty nature that defy a simple choice and may well be life-changing in their consequence;

• some of no more hurt than being left outside the candy store, looking in;

• others that can mean the difference between poverty or wealth, disease or health, death or life, years of disillusionment and despair, or years of joy and fulfillment.

Sometimes we have to struggle for a right decision, fight through long night watches weighing all the angles, wondering what to do, which way to turn, what choice to make. And just as frequently as not, once through the valley of decision, we look back in anger and regret.

Christ the Answer?

Bumper-sticker theology affirms that "Christ is the answer." What for? That depends on what the question is, and for most questions that are posed, Christ is not the answer. Common sense may be the answer. Learning gathered from the books of specialists may be the answer. Surgery or medication can often be the answer. The human brain is still the world's most marvelous computer, subject certainly to error, but built by its Creator with a thinking mechanism that cannot be duplicated. God intended us to use it, feed it, and develop it.

The Word to the Wise

But the *word to the wise* is *wisdom*. The Word to the wise is *Christ*, whom God has made our wisdom, our righteousness and sanctification and redemption.

The world cries out for wisdom. Our scientific age, with all the know-how that has been developed, cries for wisdom. Social problems that defy the best solutions we can muster cry for wisdom. The personal choices, problems, and decisions that confront us daily cry for wisdom. Who can name them all? The choice of schools and colleges, the pursuit of a career, the ethical and moral choices in relationships with others, problems that are faced and need solution in the pressure cooker of the work day world — all cry for wisdom. *We* cry for wisdom!

The Word today is taken from the Book of Proverbs, which along with Job, Ecclesiastes, and a few selected Psalms, are classified as "wisdom writings," *Kethubim* (as Hebrews called them). Their concern is rooted in the human search for wisdom and for understanding to enable us to make our way through all of life's entanglements, and with a minimum of scratches. Proverbs, in particular, provides instruction based on practical experience in everyday affairs, and as a point of interest was probably directed to young men of higher-social-class society. There are questions whether Solomon was in reality the author of the book, or whether this collection was ascribed to him as a way of honoring that great king in Judah's history. But with the emphasis on wisdom and the counsel to seek wisdom from the Lord, we are certainly reminded of the prayer of Solomon for wisdom in his own long reign as king of Israel.

Solomon's Prayer

At Gibeon the Lord appeared to Solomon by night and said, "Ask what I shall give you." As Solomon recalled the great and steadfast love that God had shown to David, and now made him to reign in David's stead, although he was "a child," he prayed for wisdom: "Give thy servant an understanding mind to govern thy people, that I may discern between good and evil: for who is able to govern this thy great people?"

It pleased the Lord that Solomon had asked this — not riches or long life, but a discerning mind. "Behold," said the Lord, "I give you a wise and discerning mind, so that none like you has been before you and none like you shall arise after you . . . I give you also what you have not asked, both riches and honor . . . and if you will walk in my ways, keeping my statutes and my commandments, then I will lengthen your days." (1 Kings 2:10-14) "And the people stood in awe of the king, because they perceived that the wisdom of God was in him, to render justice." (1 Kings 2:28)

The Word to the Wise is Wisdom, for the wise seek wisdom with a single-minded heart. The wise seek wisdom with tenacity and diligence, like the man who bought the field and plowed it to unearth the buried treasure, or the one who sought the pearl of great price. The wise importunately pray for wisdom so that they might know and choose a course of action that will prove the best in any circumstance — the "tough go" that we frequently encounter in relationships, the tough decisions and solutions that we have to make in world political affairs, and those choices that we have to make in issues neither black nor white, but rather gray. It isn't possible in every circumstance or situation to look up answers in the Bible and have every question answered. The Scripture gives us basic principles, together with the freedom and responsibility to make the choices for ourselves.

Wisdom at its Source

The Word to the Wise is Wisdom, and the wise will quickly understand that human wisdom is in short supply, not sufficient for perplexities that flow across our pathway daily. Snap judgments, quick solutions, hasty answers that deny the struggle of hard thinking will not serve. The wise seek wisdom at its source, with God — the God who in his wisdom shaped the earth, designed it and created it — the God who filled the earth with life and gave life everything it needs — the God, the only God, who could conceive the plan for human rescue from its greatest problem, sin and death, in that most amazing spectacle of Calvary.

The Word to the Wise is Wisdom, first the wisdom that can peel away illusions and mirages and see our world and all humanity as a fallen world. These are the illusions — that we can find the fountain of youth and never see death, that we can build a personal empire that will never crumble, that we can create a great society and progress to a man-made heaven, that we can mold our children in our image, that if we can set up colonies on planets we can solve the problems of world hunger.

Or what illusion is it that flashes on *your* mental image? Humanity in its own wisdom has achieved great heights, only to create another pit. We conquer one disease to be engulfed by still another. We solve one problem, only to discover we have aggravated others. The United States pursues one plan for peace, the Soviets another, only to discover that their plans for peace increase the tensions.

This is a fallen world, and these are the illusions. But the facts are that we are at odds with God. We have taken the responsibility God gave us for the care of his creation and made of it a profit motive. We have asked for our inheritance and we have made off with it to the distant pig sty. We have received the gift of life and claim it as our own. We have taken over as the little gods of our own little kingdoms and have lost the God whose kingdom we are called to serve. We are in a frantic panic, rushing headlong toward the grave, each trying to scoop up a piece of pie along the way.

The Lord Gives Wisdom

The Word to the Wise is Wisdom. "Receive my words . . . treasure up my commandments . . . attend to wisdom . . . incline your heart to understanding." Seek wisdom, struggle for it, pray for it, "for the Lord gives wisdom; from his mouth come knowledge and understanding."

The problem with the Book of Proverbs, when it is read in isolation, is that it comes out sounding strangely like a how-to manual on right living, or a secret code that opens doorways to success, property, and total personhood. But when we read it in the light of God's full counsel, the word to the wise is Christ, the living Word, the Christ whom God has made to be our wisdom. Foolishness to some, a stumbling block to others, Christ is both the power of God and the wisdom of God — God's answer to a world enshrouded in its guilt, darkened by its sin, encapsuled in death's casket. The word to the wise is Christ, in whom are hid the treasures of wisdom and knowledge. (See 1 Corinthians 1:18-31 and Colossians 2:3)

Christ -- the wisdom of God! In Christ we find salvation from a fallen world and we are given our new status as God's children once again. Let the problems now step forward to confront us, and let the puzzles pose along the way, and let us walk the valley of decisions. We are children of the heavenly Father now, free to struggle with responsibility, free to think for ourselves, and free to make an error and to know forgiving love which is the heart of wisdom.

The Word to the Wise is Christ. Then answer now, "Who are the wise?"

Proper 19 (September 11-17)
Ordinary Time 24
Proverbs 22:1-2, 8-9

The Acid Test of Wisdom

"We hold these truths to be self-evident . . .," but not as evident in fact as they are held in theory —

"That all men are created equal . . ." and while that word "men" is the inclusive language of the opening biblical salute of Genesis 1:27, some in reality are more equal than others . . .

". . . that they are endowed by their Creator with certain inalienable rights . . ." — qualified in practice to mean that unless the wheel begins to squeak, the wheel will not be greased . . .

". . . that among these are life, liberty, and the pursuit of happiness," but there seem to be some questions about the right *to* life and the rights *of* life, on whether liberty includes responsibility, and concerning what kind of "high" in happiness we dare pursue. What, if any, are the limits?

Our sojourn through the Word returns us to the ancient Book of Proverbs, the wisdom of the sages based on practical experience and often used to educate and train the coming generation of officials in the courts of kings. The Proverbs do contain wise counsel on the art of living or of piloting one's self through life. One writer on the subject likens them to "buoys that have been set out on the sea, by which one can determine one's position." Page through the Proverbs. Test them. Think them through. Then live them out, and the experience of sages will assuredly become your own. It's the experience that finds reflection in the Bill of Rights, the Declaration of Independence, and the Preamble to the Constitution of our country.

But here and there the Proverbs are much more than practical advice. Some of them address a realm of things indifferent — for instance, rules of etiquette and table manners. But in a great majority of them, in one way or another, the Proverb gives expression to the will of God. Hear this: "A good name is to be chosen rather than great riches, and favor is better than silver or gold . . . He who has a bountiful eye will be blessed, for he shares his bread with the poor." Repeatedly across the Holy Scripture, the acid test that God applies to wisdom, or to our faith, or to religion is at the point where "the rich and the poor meet together." Or the well-fed and the hungry . . . or where those who dwell in king's houses meet those who have no shelter . . . or where those who purchase on Fifth Avenue meet those who have to shop at rummage sales and church clothes closets.

The acid test of wisdom, faith, religion! What's the good of it if a brother or a sister is ill-clad, in lack of daily food, without a place to lay the head or to warm cold feet and hands, and one responds, "Good luck! I hope you find a place to eat and sleep and warm yourself"? What good is it? Faith, if it has no works, is dead, "He who has a bountiful eye will be blessed, for he shares his bread with the poor."

The acid test of wisdom, faith, religion! If a well-dressed person, decorated with gold rings and chains and bracelets, well-bathed and sprayed, should sit beside you in the pew at worship, and at your other side a poor man sharing the aroma of another kind, and you become a judge with evil thought, what good is it? "The rich and the poor meet together; the Lord is the maker of them all." That's the point where God applies the acid test.

The opening preface to the Proverbs reads, "The Proverbs of Solomon, son of David, king of Israel." (1:1) There are problems with that title and ascription, not the least of which is this that Solomon himself would hardly pass the acid test. He was the first in what has now become a long line of big spenders. He built the temple as a showplace for the nations, sparing no expense those seven years in process of construction, and then a spacious showplace for himself. He maintained seven-hundred wives, a number that has probably been rounded off, and three hundred concubines. The stables of Solomon are well known to the archeologist. They suggest that he liked horses, too, having forty-thousand of them altogether. Forced labor and heavy taxes were the order of his rule, so that Solomon in all his glory could be intact.

But down the centuries a man named Jesus would be heard to say that we would always have the poor with us, and the Israel of Solomon had its share, too — those folks to whom the wealthier could look and say, "If those people would get out and work . . . " Perhaps the proverb had a hollow ring: "He who has a bountiful eye will be blessed, for he shares his bread with the poor."

The acid test is at the point where the rich and the poor meet together, and where both understand that the Lord is the maker of them all. But frequently the paths of rich and poor run parallel and never cross. A society of capitalists has ways of segregating haves from have nots. We send our hand-me-downs downtown to clothing centers, pack a Christmas basket for the hungry, sometimes tour the pockets of poverty on get-acquainted-with-the-urban-blight excursions sponsored by the local food shelf. It's good to see and know that castoffs help. It makes us feel good when we exercise our charity.

There are signals here and there that, for many of us, our religion is a private matter. "The business of the church is saving souls." Once each week is church time, when we hold a rendezvous with God, have our souls fed, so to speak, enjoy the music and the liturgy, and now and then the sermon isn't too bad either. There is comfort in the fact that in a changing world we have a changeless church, something solid, something stable, gatherings of people like ourselves, good friends and fellowship, a blessing on the status quo. This is where we stick to our religion and keep our noses out of politics.

But the acid test permits no privacy. The church is not a spaceship we can board for trips that soar off to the seventh heaven. The church is in the world, even as its Lord was in the world, for now our Lord is in the world in us. Therefore it is said, "The church can never be too worldly!" This is where Christ's action is — among the poor, the destitute, and the deprived, at the side of those depressed and those depraved, comforting the brokenhearted, touching the diseased and healing them, breaking chains that bind the hearts of people, lifting burdens from the beaten. "Liberty and justice for all" is not reserved for an allegiance speech at civic clubs, but the banner flying over every path the Savior walked.

Especially on the highway to Jerusalem! From his ministry in Galilee, where he confronted those with various diseases, pains, paralysis, and epilepsy (signs of the demonic), Jesus went up to

Jerusalem to meet the prince of death himself. "Like a lamb led to the slaughter," he had to face the demon powers that had taken over his creation, enslaved in death grip those whose hearts were set against him. His healing love and power reached its zenith at the very place where those for whom he died, for whom he won forgiveness, for whom he purchased freedom, nailed him to the cross. Death could not destroy him nor prevent his love. The statue with the torch that stands in New York harbor runs a distant second to the cross as a symbol of liberty and justice for all. That's how it was when Jesus came to his own and his own received him not. That's how it was when the true light that enlightens everyone was coming to the world.

The light went out at Calvary for three brief days as Jesus shared the darkness of a lost humanity. But he shared it to defeat it and dispel it. That's how you and I see Calvary — his victory and our own, his light and life and love and truth restored to life again, and now the light and life and love that dwells in us. For Christ gives us his world today to live in and to love in. He lays that burden on our hearts — war ravaged nations, overcrowded cities, a plundered planet where six percent of the population consumes fifty percent of the earth's resources, where one of every three across the continents go hungry every day, and where the untold multitude still hungers for the Bread of Life.

The acid test is now applied to us.

Proper 20 (September 18-24)
Ordinary Time 25
Job 28:20-28

Ode to Wisdom

This is an Ode to Wisdom — wisdom that is not discovered in computer banks, nor taught in schools and colleges, nor learned from parents, nor symbolized in Wall Street winnings. "Where, then, shall wisdom be found? And where is the place of understanding?" (v. 12)

In this age of new enlightenment, in our high tech society, this Ode to Wisdom simply doesn't fly. When God came down from heaven to survey the Babel tower that the people back in Genesis 11 had designed, he was both amazed and amused. This colossal tower, with its head in the heavens, would become a colossal flop, just as all of our colossal towers have become since then. This symbol of human greatness would become a symbol of human folly, just as all of our greatness symbols have become since then. But when God said, "This is only the beginning of what they will do; and nothing that they propose to do will now be impossible for them," our estimate would be that even God himself could never realize how far we actually could come.

No small measure of our time and energy is invested in the praise of homo sapiens, the human species which has attained the heights and reaches for still higher heights. In contrast to the Third World nations, we see ourselves as a "developed country," and except for a commitment of concern for people ravaged by disease and undernourishment and hunger and war in poorer nations, we like it on this continent and want to stay here in the good life. We are blessed! But what have we developed in this developed country? We have much knowledge, but no wisdom. We have good answers for tough questions and well-designed solutions for hard problems, but the human puzzle remains the same. Our humanity breaks out all over as our knowledge, answers, and solutions burden us with monsters of our own making. "Where, then, shall wisdom be found? And where is the place of understanding?"

This Ode to Wisdom is discovered in the Book of Job, where, strangely, we confront a man who couldn't find it and who never found it. Because this chapter seems to jar itself upon Job's story and intrude upon its continuity, some sage students of the Scripture see it as an independent poem that was added by the author or an editor. We need not be troubled by it, for the message it conveys remains the word we need to hear. The search for wisdom is its theme — the search not one of us has ended. "Where, then, shall wisdom be found? And where is the place of understanding?"

The questions that the Book of Job has raised for every generation are the questions that have been renewed with vigor in our own — the problem of human suffering in relation to a God of justice, truth, and mercy, and in relation to our own uprightness or downrightness, or, briefly stated, "Why must the righteous suffer?" What is the problem "when bad things happen to good people," or, turned about, when good things happen to bad people?

Calamity not only rained on Job. It poured. Blessed with seven sons, three daughters, seven thousand sheep, three thousand camels, five hundred yoke of oxen, many servants, and a place of power and prestige among his neighbors, Job seemed to relish life with an abundance of God's sunshine pouring down on him. Was this the reason he "feared God" and "turned away from evil"? "God is great and God is good" when life is good and health is good and steak is on the barbeque and there are many friends with whom to eat and drink in the partying of life. But then the storm clouds gathered and the sudden devastation of the storms destroyed the man. He lost it all — his herds, his wealth, his health, his family, his friends.

Injustice! Unfair! God has to be a sadist who delights in torture! How easily one falls into the trap of charging God with harshness, cruelty, discriminate behavior, and unjust prejudice when all the gears are suddenly reversed. If we reverence God and bless him, is God not bound to bless us in return? Or if God satisfies our estimate of how he ought to bless us, and if he gives us healthy children, peaceful family life, our piece of pie, shall we not bless him in return until . . . ? The weak and immature in faith may curdle at the first faint symptom of distress. But when the symptoms multiply, the sprinkle turns to showers and the showers turn to thunderstorms and thunderstorms develop into hurricanes, even the strongest of our company are shaken to the core. It takes a heaping Spirit-full to face disaster in the faith of Habakkuk, "Though the fig tree do not blossom, nor fruit be on the vines, the produce of the olive fail and no food in the fields, the flock be cut off from the fold and no herd in the stalls, yet I will rejoice in the Lord, I will joy in the God of my salvation."

A younger mother in my parish can recall the day I visited just after her first child was born.

"God was surely with me," this young mother said. "I had an easy time delivering, the care was good, a loving husband was at hand, and my little girl is healthy, perfect, and well formed and really pretty." And she recalls how she resented it when I responded,

"Susan, God is always with his children. He was with you in this blessing, and he would have been with you if everything had not gone as you wanted it."

"At the moment I was much too young and had too many answers — wrong ones — to understand," she now admits and thanks me for the sudden jolt in growth.

An old favorite says it this way:

Though he giveth or he taketh,
God his children ne'er forsaketh;
His the loving purpose solely
To preserve them pure and holy.

Job, too, was surrounded by counselors in his distress and anguish. Whenever all the walls close in and we are crushed between them, counselors will be at hand like sages with the answers to the riddles. They will probe the hidden side of wisdom and come up with counsel which, if we are wise, we have to follow. "I think . . . " or "In my opinion . . . " or "experience has taught me that . . . " — these comments flow like water from the bubbler of eternal wisdom. But finally the person in the pit will have to struggle through alone. Eliphaz, Bildad, and Zophar — those were Job's good friends and counselors. Who are yours? Sometimes the counselors are in reality the enemy.

It is in the setting of this book, then, that the Ode to Wisdom suddenly appears, a shining jewel in the darkness, picking up one ray of light and boldly beaming it to make its presence known. It serves as closure to the dialogue of Job with Eliphaz, Bildad, and Zophar, a summary of Job's best confidence that wisdom can be found not in our own achievement, but as a gift of God. Wisdom never comes as a result of our own effort, but only as God gives it and God speaks it. "Whence then comes wisdom? And where is the place of understanding?"

Let this be known. "It is hid from the eyes of all living, and concealed from the birds of the air." Our deepest insights cannot reach it. Abaddon, which means "destruction," and death cannot provide it, for they have only heard a rumor of it on the gossip wires of the pretense people.

But "God understands the way to it, and he knows its place." Wisdom was at hand when God's creation wonder was in progress, and wisdom is at hand in his continuing creation process. Wisdom is the principle behind all other principles in God's design. And wisdom is the principle we need to know behind that great design expressed today in St. Mark's Gospel, where the word is given: "The Son of man will be delivered into the hands of men, and they will kill him, and when he is killed, after three days he will rise."

This would scarcely be called wisdom in the laboratories of human progress or in the office of your broker or in the greater halls of learning or in the court of human rights. It is not "a wisdom of this age or of the rulers of this age, who are doomed to pass away. It is the secret and hidden wisdom of God, which God decreed before the ages for our glorification. None of the rulers of this age understood this; for if they had, they would not have crucified the Lord of glory. But, as it is written, 'What no eye has seen, nor ear heard, nor the heart of man conceived, what God has prepared for those who love him,' God has revealed to us through the Spirit." (1 Corinthians 2:6b-10a)

Whence, then, comes wisdom? And where is the place of understanding? "Behold, the fear of the Lord, that is wisdom; and to depart from evil is understanding."

The struggle didn't end for Job, of course, at that point. It never ends that simply. Reverence for the Lord is only the beginning of the struggle, at the very point where one has tired of it altogether. The struggle starts where Christ lays hold on us, Wisdom in the flesh, and turns our footsteps to the cross — both his, and ours. The jealousy and the ambition hole up in the hearts of men like Judas, Caiaphas, and Pontius Pilate, who choose to bear the burden of their guilt while those who walk The Way amidst scorn and shame and sacrifice find crucifixion soon becomes their new creation. Their new life may not have all the answers, and their problems may not find a quick fix, and the riddles of existence may not easily be solved or ever solved, but they have Christ!

Proper 21 (September 25 — October 1)
Ordinary Time 26
Job 42:1-6

Questions Without Answers

The Word today is the bottom line in the Book of Job, the story of the man from the land of Uz who was blameless and upright and who feared God and turned away from evil. The man had prospered. He had seven sons and three daughters, seven thousand sheep, three thousand camels, five hundred yoke of oxen, five hundred she-asses and very many servants. We could say that he belonged to the affluent society, a rather rare type in his day because the record makes it clear that he was the greatest man of all the people in the East.

We will take the Book at its word, but how anyone who is blameless and upright and fears God and turns away from evil can revel in prosperity like that while half the world is starving is beyond the mind. Across the chapters of his story, there is not much to suggest that he was any great philanthropist, that he endowed a university, gave matching funds to a humanitarian cause, or had a city park named after him. Let's just say that there is much about the Book of Job that we will never understand. There is also much Job didn't understand.

Why?

The question that seems to surface through this Word today is one that rides the surface of life continually when the fish aren't biting and the day is not right, "Why must the righteous suffer?" The contemporary way of saying it is, "Why do bad things happen to good people?" You remember that strange dialogue between the

Lord and Satan, during which Satan asked, "Have you not bestowed on Job your special favor, thrown a hedge around him and his house, blessed his labors, multiplied his wealth?"

"You see, God." Satan said, "Job finds that you are a successful God, and he enjoys success, but if you strip him down to nothing, put a question mark behind your operation, then watch what he will do. He will soon come over into my camp, and he will curse you to your face."

So this is what God did: He gave Satan his permission to afflict Job, strip him of his wealth, destroy his children and his cattle and his servants, and afflict him with disease that drove him out of his skin. And this is what Job did: He cursed the day he was born. His wife had counseled him to curse God, too, and then go hang himself, but Job as a God-fearing man could not quite bring himself to that.

There are some great and faith-filled statements scattered through the Book of Job. Like these, for example:

"The Lord gave and the Lord has taken away. Blessed be the name of the Lord."

"Shall we receive good at the hand of God, and shall we not receive evil?"

Or that great masterpiece in 19:25:

"I know that my Redeemer lives, and at last he will stand upon the earth."

There are also some assuring statements:

"Happy is the man whom God reproves; therefore, despise not the chastening of the Almighty . . . (Job 5:17) You shall know that your tent is safe." (Job 5:24)

And there are also statements of despair:

"Man is born to trouble as the sparks fly upward." (Job 5:7)

But the thread that ties it all together is the search for answers.

The haunting question that repeats itself throughout Job's story is the question, "Why?"

The story speaks to those big questions that have always puzzled people — the questions of disease and pain, reverse and suffering. It takes the answers we have usually devised and tears them into shreds. It gathers up all our easy answers, the ones we use for our defenses, and peels them back. Our neat categories and well-ordered files: it tips them over and dumps them out. Snappy clichés get caught between the teeth, like "God helps those who help themselves." Our tongues are twisted on those pretzels.

Counsel

Job had three friends who offered counsel. Some of it was not bad, but certainly not satisfying either. It was better counsel than we often hear in mortuary parlors when our friends come in to comfort, saying, "Cheer up! Chin up!" What a mockery! Or worse: "We must accept this as the will of God. It could have been much worse. Just think. He might have lived, but he would not have been the same." That's the problem, isn't it? What *is* the will of God?

Advise and Consent

Who has known the mind of the Lord? (Romans 11:34) Not one of us, and that's for sure. But it's amazing, isn't it, how many of us with our simple answers seem to have God figured out and psychoanalyzed and know exactly what he is up to. Those pyschic powers that we use to read the hearts of friends or enemies, interpret actions, pass cute judgments — we exercise those psychic powers on God, too. Our question, "Why?" becomes our charge against him: capricious, unjust, unfair. Perhaps he suffers from dementia praecox or schizophrenia.

Or who has been his counselor? (Romans 11:34) Many of us brazenly and openly seek that appointment to his inner circle of advisers. If we could have a place around the table in the Oval Office, help determine policy, advise and consent, the operation would be smoother than it is, more sensitive to human rights and civil rights and constitutional rights. We would be less likely to get into trouble with the Civil Liberties Union. It doesn't take much legal savvy, does it, to observe that every right Job had was violated by God's behavior. Job should have his day in court.

Take God to Court

We can multiply the instances when we would like to get God into court, when we could prosecute him for the violation of our rights, find him guilty, sentence him to solitary out in outer space where his disturbances cannot affect us. It's an awful thing to say! But when his disturbances reach into our own family circles, or when "accident" deprives us of our fullest life, or when disease strikes out of nowhere, we can think those things, if not burst out to say them. A bit of trouble here and there, a little setback now and then may not be difficult. We can take it and attribute it in noble spirit to the chastening of God. But when it rains and pours and the floodtide of adversity reaches our chin level, is that a scream we hear?

God's Turn

But hurry now. Get on to chapter 38. I think God has to get a little "sick and tired," if I dare to say it that way, of our endless questions and analysis and judgments, and the way we try to justify ourselves, defend ourselves, preserve our rights, demand our day in court with him. After nearly everyone had had his say — Job's counselors and friends and Job himself — God had *his* say. Whoever it was that divided Scripture into chapter and verse allows three chapters for the pummeling Job had to take. Seventy-one sharp questions God hit him with, as God threw Job on the defensive. I like the color in the way Fred Buechner put it: "Just the way God cleared his throat almost blasted Job off his feet."*

"Who is this that darkens counsel by words without knowledge? Gird up your loins. Stand up like a man. It's my turn now to question you, and you had better answer!" And then the cross examination started. What a burn! "Who are you to question me? Were you around when heaven and earth were made? Did you establish its foundations? Were you there to hear the concert when the morning stars sang together, and all the sons of God shouted

Frederick Buechner, *Peculiar Treasures,* p. 68.

for joy? Have you commanded the morning since your days began and caused the dawn to know its place?''

Racing from one question to another, scarcely pausing for a breath, God with his little hammer at the heart drove Job into a corner. And that's not too wise either, is it, for we in our smarts know what happens when you corner a cat. We win no friends that way.

Repentance

But whatever God intended, he accomplished. Job confessed to his stupidity, to talking out of turn, to playing expert on the things he didn't understand. ''I had heard about you all my life. But it is now no longer second-hand reports. It is my personal experience. I have heard you with my ear, and I have seen you with my eyes. Therefore I abhor myself in dust and ashes.''

And now my social worker friends begin to squint and squirm. To abhor myself in dust and ashes does nothing for my self-esteem. A high self-image is important to a high and healthy life and attitude. But what we often call a good self-image isn't high enough. That which drags us down needs first of all to be dragged out. That which gets between our own self-image and the image God wants us to share must first be swept aside.

Said Peter on the shores of Galilee, ''Depart from me. I am a sinful man, O Lord.'' Said Isaiah in his vision of the holy throne and smoking temple, ''Woe is me, for I am lost; I am a man of unclean lips, and I dwell in the midst of a people of unclean lips; for my eyes have seen the King, the Lord of hosts.'' Said Job here in the Word today, ''But now my eye sees thee; therefore I despise myself, and repent in dust and ashes.''

It is, in fact, in that repentance that Job realized he was a creature, not creator, and in that repentance that God brought the word to Job for his day and the grace that Job received. And when Job's story closes, Job still has no answers. He has more than answers. He has God!

The Final Word is Christ

In this Christian congregation, what is it that we look for when the riddles and the puzzles and the problems and the questions line up on the path of life, each one more defiant than the one before? Solutions? Answers? Mysteries revealed, all the puzzles finally unraveled? Explanations? We have need for none of them. For our eyes have seen the brightest splendor that has ever been revealed, the one that isn't even mentioned through the Book of Job. We have been to Calvary. We have seen God break his heart with suffering we can never comprehend and in a mystery of grace that we can never penetrate. If he did that for us, dare we ask, "Why?"

Proper 22 (October 2-8)
Ordinary Time 27
Genesis 2:18-24

The Marriage of Adam and Eve

This is how it started! It happened long ago and far away, in a place called Eden (Eden Prairie to the southwest of Minneapolis bears no resemblance to it), that the masculine and feminine were joined together as complement (not compliment) for each other . . . that the man became a husband and the woman became a wife . . . that the differences between the sexes formed a blend of unity and love.

This is how it started! The ceremony was unique, performed amid the most unusual circumstances: no bridal gown, no tuxedo, no officiating or officious clergyperson, no processional music other than the song of birds and harmonies of a perfect creation. There had been no previous pre-marital examinations as a preparation. There had been no marriage license application at the office of the Eden County clerk, no waiting period. There had not even been a time of trial to test compatibility, a period of courtship, an opportunity to practice sex, or in any sense to play the game of Romeo and Juliet.

This is how it started! They were married in the great cathedral of creation by an act of God's creating love. And they lived happily ever after!?

If we would know, however, how it really started, we cannot begin that day in Eden when God anesthetized the man, took a rib, and had him wake up to a woman. It began before that in the heart of the Creator God when in the last and most mysterious of kindnesses he would bestow, he designed the counterpart and complement — someone like him, yet not identical to him — a counterpart of equal rank. This was the crowning act of goodness in a series of creative kindnesses that God designed.

"It is not good that the man should be alone!" It is not good that the man should think of no one but himself, seeking nothing but his own, be self-contained in his own "rights." There has to be another. So God created woman, brought her to the man, and immediately he recognized and greeted her as one with him, of equal rank, "bone of my bones and flesh of my flesh." And *eros* was born, the power of the sexual drive implanted by our God himself. The relationship of man and woman had been given dignity — the miracle and mystery of God's creation.

It started, therefore, in the goodness of the heart of God's intention for creation. His design was Life, the Life Abundant! The gifts of *eros,* sexuality, and marriage were designed for happiness, companionship, continuing creation as the man and woman came together in their children, sharing totally.

Original Design is Lost

But we are living in a fallen world. The innocence of Eden, where the man and woman both were naked and were not ashamed, is now behind us. The original design is lost. The perfection of creation with its unity and beauty is destroyed. And "holy marriage" has become the victim of our interference with the rule of God as we set out to rule each other.

Adam and Eve did not live happily ever after. One needs only turn a page to learn that the honeymoon was over; the holy wedlock had become a deadlock as the man is heard to say in shame, "The woman whom you gave me . . . "

We are all familiar with the story — not with Adam's story, not with Eve's (we don't know what all might have happened there), but with our own — the story that is most familiar. There is not a one of us who has not played the lead role — whether we are married now, or whether we are not, or whether we are yet to be or not to be. The desire to be God was Adam's fall, and Eve's and it is ours — both with marriage and without it, although the ugliness of "personal rights insistence" probably breaks loose in no more tender place than marriage.

Now the purposes of marriage have been fouled — a way to "legalize" the bed, to satisfy the urge and be respectable about it;

or for many in our time, a stifling way of life to be avoided lest they cross the forty mark without their fair share of variety, experience, and personal thrill. With consciences anesthetized, their preference is to sleep around, or shack up without commitment, until one morning they awaken to an image in the mirror of a wasted face, a wasted life, and one discarded on the wreckage heap of junkers.

Made for Each Other

Go back a moment into Eden when Adam was alone. Our Lord had formed the beasts and birds and every living creature, a world that teemed with life and beauty, and in the midst of all that life one special life. There was a parade one day, when God paraded all his living creatures before Adam to receive a name, and whatever Adam called the creature, that would be its name. But there was something missing on the scene, for in all that host of creatures, there was none like Adam — none to love, to share with, and to live for.

"It is not good that man should be alone. I will make a helper fit for him." And so it was, right there, that God accomplished this fantastic marvel of creation and presented her to Adam. We are privileged to tune in on his praise:

"This is now my very self."

Man and woman — they were not made for themselves. They were made for each other.

The Key

The emphasis today is on the "personal" — personal fulfillment, personal identity, personal role, and personal satisfaction — as though each one of us were all alone and no one mattered.

"It is not good that the man (or woman) should be alone."

We express it in our jargon: "I gotta do my thing!" (From this, dear Lord, deliver us.) Or in Sinatra's song: "I did it my way." (What a way to go!) Or in another wistful melody that rebels against conformity: "I gotta be me!" (What sort of goal in life is that?)

But experience becomes conviction that no one ever finds fulfillment, happiness, or satisfaction when the self becomes the goal. No one can love another certainly without a healthy self-respect and measure of self-love. Did Archie Bunker *really* love himself as much as he pretended? Why, then, was he angry all the time? Why the need to sit in judgment over anyone whose style or color was a little different shade? Did not Archie really hate himself and find it necessary to use fig leaves as a covering against the icy chill of his own ego, scarred by self-hate. To love one's self is to be free from need for fig leaves and defenses and whatever style of cover-up we choose. Self-respect or self-esteem or self-love is the key to love for others.

And the gift of marriage as a gift of love from God is precisely that — the intimate commitment of one's self to that one person God has given us, for in fulfilling that commitment we are ourselves fulfilled.

Marriage goes all wrong when it becomes that "noble fifty-fifty" proposition, or when it means a built-in mistress for the husband or a built-in chore boy for the wife, or when it becomes the private empire where each spouse has a personal agenda that is so well hidden even from him/herself — the agenda of self-seeking. The honeymoon is over then. The Hilton bridal suite becomes the penthouse sour.

Idealism to Realism

Be sure of this! The story back in Genesis is not another version of the marriage dream — the fairy tale of prince and princess who found happiness forever. Every pastor at the altar has seen the starry-eyed, love-blinded couples on their happy day. They were full of optimism and idealism and enthusiasm. That's a joy, of course, and we would like to see much more of it. But soon idealism is replaced by realism. The dream world of the wedding day becomes the real world of the marriage with adjustments, differences, and conflicts.

The Gospel of our Lord is meant for this! It is meant for couples in a fallen world who struggle with the gift of marriage because they struggle with themselves. The Gospel of our Lord is meant for this — to bind our hearts together through the tensions and the conflicts with forgiving love. The Gospel of our Lord is meant for this — to speak forgiveness from the cross and tomb. The Savior who was offered up for our transgressions, raised again for our salvation, comes to live with us, to love with us, to teach forgiveness as the oil that smooths relationships. His Word, "I love you," is the Gospel word that energizes love for him and for each other. There is no other way.

The Word We Need

This is the word we need to turn to regularly if the love that we have known in Jesus Christ is to become the love we know for one another — this same self-sacrificing love. "Husbands, love your wives, as Christ loved the church and gave himself up for her." "Wives, see that you reverence your husbands," even as the church, redeemed with Jesus' blood, must reverence her Lord. The Gospel of the grace of God in Christ is good news, not only the power of God to salvation, but also the power of God for the salvation of holy marriage. It enables us to live as children of the heavenly Father. It enables us to live in love. It enables us to live in freedom. It enables us to build each other in the faith so that we can live in that calm confidence that around us and beneath us are the everlasting arms of him who gave himself for us.

In a day when countless marriages collapse and countless homes are shredded and the spirits of a million children are left battered as the victims, many marriage manuals have been written as the how-to rules for a successful marriage. Perhaps they have been helpful. They can also be demonic and deceptive.

Have you noticed how, when you have read a paragraph from one of them, you want to read it to your spouse to shape your wife or husband in the mold the manual suggests? There is always the temptation to make rules and standards of behavior for the other person, shape him up, or her, build the fences, change his ways, or hers, but "life under law" has never worked. "Life in rules" does not afford a life of love. The marriage manual God has given us has just one word — *Christ*.

Christ is the word for severed marriages as well, for people who made terrible mistakes and need desperately to be forgiven. Christ does not chain us to our errors. He unwraps the chains and sets us free and brings us back across the path of penitence to our forgiving Father, and to grace!

It is no accident that in his parables and in his images our Lord used marriage as an illustration of his intimate relationship with us — Christ the bridegroom and his church the bride, and the marriage feast a symbol for the joy of everlasting life. He has given us the treasured gift of marriage and all the gifts that marriage carries with it — home and family and sexuality; forgiveness, love, security. But in the best of gifts he gives himself.

40

Proper 23 (October 9-15)
Ordinary Time 28
Genesis 3:8-19

Man, Where Are You?

The story of the fall of Adam and Eve disturbs a lot of people, raises many questions, and poses many problems. How can anyone who lives in this advanced society with our advanced technology and our unlimited horizons believe in talking serpents?

• Or with our advanced theology how are we to understand a God who hangs our fate in trees?

• Or when we have passed the finals and the orals and have gained all wisdom and all knowledge, how can anybody be this stupid?

• Or how could God be so harsh as to impose these stiff penalties and even sentence us to death for one naughty little no-no?

If you pull the cover back a little farther, the disturbance deepens. We discover that it isn't a talking serpent that perplexes us, but what he says that gets to us. And suddenly it isn't Adam and his partner Eve whose names are on the marquee of the world theater as the leading actors, but our names that are blazing in the lights, and each of us is in the leading role. We begin to see that certain scenes in our lives are repeated in the story and we recognize the naked male and female who, in their embarrassment, are hiding in the bushes, trying on the latest style in fig leaves. We recognize the voice that we hear strolling through the garden in the cool of the day, for we have heard it many times ourselves (if we have not destroyed the conscience altogether): "Man, where are you?"

The Fall

The story is disturbing to a world of people — not the story, really, but the happening reported, which in the language of the church is called "The Fall." And it isn't the event as Eve and Adam perpetrated it, but the event as you and I have duplicated it, not their stupidity, but ours that bugs us. Adam's fall and ours, his event and our events are concentrated here.

The event? The imperishable has put on the perishable; the immortal has put on mortality; the holy has clothed himself in unholiness; life has absorbed itself in death. The perfect world of God's creation has been turned to turmoil, the harmony to enmity. The plan of God is overshadowed by the schemes of people. Where nature was to be a friend to people, it became an enemy. Where people were designed as stewards, they became exploiters. Where they were meant to live in love and peace and fellowship with one another, they began to fight each other, looking out for number one. Perhaps we need to be reminded here that this name "Adam" is the Hebrew word for *man* and "Eve," the *mother of all living*. So "Man" — that could be any many or woman or child — it could be your name, my name, too — "Man, where are you?"

"Man, where are you?" Are you walking in the strength of God, deploying as your weapons Word and Promise and the power of prayer? Or are you walking on the cutting edges of temptation?

No Different

The woman and the man in Eden were no different from the woman and the man at your house and the place where you have tilled the soil of pleasant living. Those for whom one does the most are often those who turn to do one in. God had done everything for this first pair, but as they walked the cutting edges of temptation, they not only scorned the power of God, they challenged it. That's what the fall is all about.

The concept of temptation has been loaded with the baggage of misunderstanding. We think of Satan's tempting lures as opportunities for peccadilloes that make life interesting and exciting. We associate temptation with the passionate desire to get involved with the forbidden, pluck the fruit, kick over traces and go out to do what we were not supposed to do. It certainly involves all that — the sins of greed and lust and hatred, with their promises of better things for us.

But temptation means much more than this. It's the constant crisis of our lives. It's the yearning to be free of God and on our own. It's being always on the point of going over to the enemy. And that temptation isn't on a baited hook that someone dangles like a lure before our eyes. It's on the inside that the prod to outlaw God is felt. Sometimes it comes disguised as piety, or in questions that concern our daily needs, or in lust for power and success, pride and self-esteem, the knowledge we have gained, our role in life. It appeals where the appeal is felt most strongly — from within the heart.

"Man, where are you?" Are you walking in the strength of God, deploying the resources he has given in his Word and Promise and the offer of the power we can tap in prayer? If temptation is the constant crisis of our lives and if we walk in danger all the way, we have no other help except to walk with Jesus all the way. If this is where the action is, at the very heart and core of life, where there is nothing that cannot be used to separate me from the love of God, then it is here within the heart that Christ must dwell. I need to taste the grief he knows when I go other ways. I need to tap the surging strength that Christ employed when he confronted Satan in the wilderness and routed him.

I remember friends of mine in childhood, children of a pastor near my father's parish in Wisconsin. Their dad surrounded them with prohibitions, so that many things that I was free to do or take or leave were not permitted them. They lived inside high fences built with rules and law, designed to keep the wolves of hell away from them and make them walk the straight and narrow. Much less restaining, my own father operated with the Gospel. He could not build fences that would keep the world away. No fences could be high enough, because the world is not out there. It is here within the heart. The opportunities to sin are not out there. They are in here. So Dad's goal was not to build the fences that would keep the world away, but to fill my heart with Christ who would enable me to sift the world — be in it, yet not of it. Today I thank him for his trust, not in his son, but in God's Son. I confess that Dad was often disappointed in his son, but never disappointed in the Son of God. And if he asked, as often he would have to ask, "Son, where are you?" he expected me to answer, "Standing in the strength of Christ, my Lord!"

Some may have seen the Hollywood extravaganza of a few years back entitled *Gandhi*. You may recall that following a fast, as Gandhi was recovering, the woman from America who had been given access to his life as a photographer and newsperson, heard him speak to this effect: "The only war one needs to fight is against the devils within the heart." She asked,

"And how are you doing in that battle, Mr. Gandhi?"

And he answered, "Not very well. That's why I'm tolerant of others."

My quotation my not be exactly accurate, for memory lacks precision. But it was touché to many Christians who have never learned.

"Man, where are you?" Are you walking in the strength of God? Are you on a guilt trip, or are you walking in forgiveness?

The Blame Game

As the voice of God came walking in the garden and called out, "Man, where are you?" God's first pair of children hid themselves. They were by no means arrogant enough to say, "Dear God, there has been a breakdown. Your creation didn't work right. You didn't build the fences high enough. Besides, we're only human. You made us this way, don't you know?"

Instead, they ran for cover, for they knew that what they ought to say was what the Psalmist said a few years later: "Against thee, thee only, have I sinned. Miserere nobis."

But finally they got around to it — the blame game! The guilt! The guilt! Who has the guilt! And you know where the blame was placed.

"The woman whom you gave me!"

"The serpent whom you put in Paradise."

"You! God! You!"

Do you now insist that this is just a myth? We say the same thing, don't we?

"I, a poor, miserable sinner. We are by nature sinful and unclean."

Someone in a moment of rebellion said it this way: "I can understand how people can forgive each other, and even understand that God could forgive people, but what I'll never understand is how God can forgive himself." We try everything to handle guilt, even laying it on God himself.

Lay the Guilt on God

Laying it on God himself?

Well, if you feel that your heart with its fig leaves, or your plastic front, has been penetrated, listen! What else will you do with guilt?

It isn't that we lay it on him. Instead, it's that he takes it on himself. From the moment of the fall, God took the guilt upon himself.

The only way one can get off the hook is when Christ gets him off the hook. And the only way Christ gets us off the hook is when one understands that one is on the hook. The first step, then, is to acknowledge guilt. Harry Truman had a sign, they tell us, saying that, "The buck stops here." Well, man, where are you?

"I'm on the hook, Lord. Only you can get me off."

That's why the promise came so quickly on the heels of human sin — the promise of a seed to crush the serpent's head and send him reeling to defeat. And we have seen the promise kept. We have seen Christ Jesus. We no longer need to hide behind the fig leaves. We can be honest. He will not despise us or reject us, guilty as we are. He forgives us. He loves us. He defends us.

We are walking in the grace of God's forgiveness.

"Man, where are you?" In the midst of death, or life? Mortality, or immortality? A temporary flash across the stage, or in eternal life?

"In the day you eat, you die!" That's what he said.

But we say, "Surely not. It can't be all that bad."

Then how do we account for this: a world that has become a walking graveyard, full of skeletons with rattling bones and empty hearts and broken hopes, still trying, each of us, to reach the stars as number one? Or what other "social problem" would you like to name?

"Man, where are you?"

Well, if you would like to know, I'm in the midst of life, enjoying life — in Christ. The way is his, and it's a thrill to see the great surprises that he brings to me along the way and how he works for our eternal good. My time is his, so I have time along the way to reach out to a sister who is hungry with a loaf of bread and with the bread of life. My life is Christ's and that means I'm secure and safe, and I can risk my life for him.

This we affirm when we deploy the Word and Promise and the power of God. Then we are strong in the Lord and in the power of his might. We are clothed in his armor — the shield of faith, the helmet of salvation, the sword of the Spirit.

Bring on the devil. Christ is ready.

Proper 24 (October 16-22)
Ordinary Time 29
Isaiah 53:7-12

The Heart of The Gospel

*[While the following sermon may be adapted to the usual solo style
of the parish parson, it could also be used in the more dramatic
form. The copy indicates a role for seven resonant voices,
strategically placed at various locations in the church, not visible to
the congregation. The lines should be carefully rehearsed so that
they are spoken with effective accent, and in a manner that flows
with the body of the sermon.]*

If Jesus Christ had won his case, he would have lost the world.
He lost his case and won the world.

*(First voice) "It was the will of the Lord to bruise him; he has
put him to grief."*

In the struggle, agony, and blood sweat of Gethsemane he
begged for clemency and pleaded for relief.

*(Second voice) "My Father, if it be possible, let this cup pass
from me; nevertheless, not as I will, but as thou wilt."*

At the palace of the high priest, Caiaphas, although the
testimony of the witness was obviously false, Jesus offered no
defense. Silence. And Caiaphas, in a theatric show of piety and
righteous wrath, tore his robes and screamed,

*(Third voice) "You have heard his blasphemy. What is your
judgment?"*

And they answered, "He deserves death!"

If Jesus Christ had won his case, he would have lost the world. He lost his case and won the world.

At the judgment seat of Pontus Pilate, in the civil court of Caesar's Roman Empire, accused by the ecclesiastics, forsaken by his own disciples, left to face the wrath and mockery of enemies alone, Jesus gave no answers.

(First voice) "He was oppressed and he was afflicted, yet he opened not his mouth. Like a lamb that is led to the slaughter, and like a sheep that before its shearers is dumb, so he opened not his mouth."

And finally the civil ruler washed his hands of the affair, pronounced the sentence of conviction on the Christ, and in the irony of the enigma, salvation's word for all the world was heard,

(First voice) "His blood be on us and our children."

(Second voice) "By oppression and judgment he was taken away, cut off out of the land of the living, stricken for the transgression of his people, and he made his grave with the wicked."

They put an end to him, but he had given to his world a new beginning.

(First voice) "Therefore I will divide him a portion with the great . . . because he poured out his soul to death, and was numbered with the transgressors; yet he bore the sin of many."

If Jesus Christ had won his case, he would have lost the world. He lost his case, and won the world.

You remember how it was when in the desert place, our Lord for forty days prepared to take those steadfast steps toward Calvary. And the devil took him to the mountain to show him all the kingdoms of the world, and the glory of them, and the devil said to him,

(Fourth voice) "All these I will give you, if you will fall down

and worship me.''

But Jesus said,

(Second voice) "Begone, Satan! For it is written, 'You shall worship the Lord your God and him only shall you serve.' ''

Accent that word "serve." When will we ever learn?

When he stood at Gabbatha and gazed intently once again into the eyes of Satan, this time reflected in the pupils of the eyes of Pontus Pilate; when the cross that he would bleed on, suffer on, and die on before the sunset of that day could scarcely look like anything that might be called a kingdom, Pilate's question must have struck him like a bolt of lightning,

(Fifth voice) "Are you a king then?''

And perhaps there was a flashback to that mountain in the desert and the kingdoms of the world spread out before him. There could be no doubt about it, that a cross is not a fit throne for a king. A castoff purple robe is hardly king's apparel. A crown of thorns, its needles pointing downward, drawing blood, is surely not a royal crown. Death by crucifixion is not the way kings go to win a kingdom, much less the world. Therefore, what mockery is this?

(First voice) "It was the will of the Lord to bruise him; he has put him to grief; when he makes himself an offering for sin, he shall see his offspring, he shall prolong his days; the will of the Lord shall prosper in his hand; he shall see the fruit of the travail of his soul and be satisfied.''

(Second voice) "He shall make many to be accounted righteous; he shall bear their iniquities.''

If Jesus Christ had won his case, he would have lost the world. He lost his case and won the world.

None of us has ever walked in Jesus' sandals. We have never known a destiny like Golgotha. We can never comprehend the burden that he carried when he bore upon his holy heart and in his spirit the iniquity of all the world, when he became the lightning rod of heaven's wrath for everything that had gone wrong in God's creation. None of us has ever known the pain of crucifixion. To attempt to calculate his burden would be more impossible than an attempt to understand the national debt.

Each of us, of course, has carried personal burdens. Some may have known a time when life seemed cut off from the land of the living, and even God seemed to have turned his face from us, and closed his ears to us, and from the pits of a living hell we cried in vain. Trusted friends had turned against us. False witness on poison wires of a telephone had spread like prairie fire through the circle of acquaintances. We stood before a bench with many judges, each of them the picture of disdain and condemnation.

A faithful pastor friend of mine became the scapegoat for the problems of his parish — a not-at-all-unusual experience for pastors. His central city parish had not grown like Schuller's crystal empire. Folks couldn't always stomach claims the Gospel laid on them. At times he crossed wrong-minded individuals or stepped on toes that wanted to be tickled. Antagonists came out from woodwork like cockroaches in a kitchen. An evangelism board that had neglected its evangelism, a stewardship committee that had never met and much less worked, a board of elders that could make no claim except that they were elder — all flicked their ashes in his face. Those with whom the pastor had become the closest as he bore their burdens with them suddenly became most distant. Those for whom he worked the hardest suddenly became his hardest work. So he bore the sin and the neglect of many. He was driven from his ministry by that demonic power that makes vultures out of saints.

However tragic our experience, not one of us can possibly approach what Christ endured. We can only stand in awe that finally must burst with praise. We have the Gospel here, the very heart of it, in this familiar chapter from Isaiah's prophecy. For what it simply tells us is that this strange way of going, this way of non-success, when it is measured by our human standards, was *for us*. He wore the crown of thorns so that we might enjoy the crown of life. He wore the purple robe of mockery to give us robes of righteousness. He suffered the defeat of death to share with us the victory of eternal life. We cannot comprehend that either, can we? He doesn't really ask us for our understanding. He asks our faith. God hangs his Word on this — his Promise.

"His blood be on us and on our children?" Yes! "The blood of Jesus Christ, his son, cleanses us from all sin."

"It was the will of the Lord to bruise him?" Yes! "He was wounded for our transgressions; he was bruised for our iniquities."

"He was stricken for the transgression of my people?" Yes! "He was put to death for our trespasses and raised for our justification."

Because Christ lost his case, he won the world. And God gives us the victory through our Lord Jesus Christ.

That changes our perspectives, doesn't it? The intensity with which we try to win our case, our ego trips and quest for greatness, our aversion to criticism and our passion for applause, using Jesus as a pad against the shocks of life, or a ladder for successful living, or as a way of satisfying our own personal need — all these are perspectives that are out of focus.

Remember James and John?

(Sixth voice) "Lord, we want you to do for us whatever we ask."

(Seventh voice) "Grant us to sit, one at your right hand and one at your left, in your glory."

The request is not so much concerned about the seating arrangements in heaven as it is about the scramble for the place of honor in the church. We will "serve the Lord with gladness" if we are duly recognized. Carelessness with fragile egos, forgetfulness in gracious handling of the recognition ceremonies, failure to build platforms for the social climbers — these are just a few of the division points in countless congregations.

A young person of my acquaintance, studying for ministry, told the bishop of the church that she could not give everything she had to that profession. She had her own needs, too, and her own time to be protected, and her own goals to be pursued.

"You do not know what you are asking," Jesus said. "Are you able to drink the cup that I drink, or to be baptized with the baptism with which I am baptized?"

(Second voice) "Whoever would be first among you must be slave of all. Whoever would be great among you must be your servant."

My favorite Bible scholars are those who guide me through Isaiahs' prophecies. They tell me that Isaiah 53 must be included in the list of Servant Songs with which that prophecy is loaded. They also tell me that the precise identity of the "servant" is an elusive one — whether it is Israel as a nation, or Israel at some point in her history, or the prophet in his own experience. Certainly it is one of the most clearly spoken prophecies of Christ and the New Covenant in all of the Old Covenant.

But if we are Christ's, I trust that now, from here on out, there is no further doubt about it. Do you recognize the servant now?

Are you prepared to drink the cup and be baptized with his baptism? If any would come after me, let him deny himself, take up his cross, and follow me. The heart of the Gospel becomes the Gospel in our hearts.

Proper 25 (October 23-29)
Ordinary Time 30
Jeremiah 31:7-9

The Lord Has Saved His People

Perhaps this is the best that I can offer you today as good news in a world of grizzled news, this shout of praise from Jeremiah's lips: "The Lord has saved his people." "Sing aloud with gladness for Jacob, and raise shouts for the chief of the nations; proclaim, give praise, and say, 'The Lord has saved his people.'"

But it seems to this observer who is more than casual in his observing that the church has punctuated Jeremiah's praise with question marks instead of exclamation points. "The Lord has saved his people?" Has he, indeed? Do we look like God's saved people? Do we march with confidence and courage and conviction to our mission? Do we radiate the gladness of salvation? Or has our faith become the dull routine and grind of following the rule book, with carefully designed allowances for failures?

Can You Hang On?

Pointedly I want to ask, "Can you hang onto that?" Regardless of the circumstance of life, no matter what, can you hang onto that, "The Lord has saved his people"? When everything your life has known or hoped for threatens to collapse, when there is no phoenix promising to rise from ashes, when your little world becomes a deep, dark forest in the gloom of night with specters lurking all about you, and when you, who always wanted to insist that you could manage your own life, can manage it no longer, can you hang onto that "The Lord has saved his people"?

I read somewhere not long ago that a person cannot really know the faithfulness of God unless one sees it in the faithfulness of people. Too bad, then about the faithfulness of God, for where, indeed, are faithful people? How could one believe that there's a Father who is heavenly when one's own father is so earthly? Or what is so great about God giving up his Son when it has become a national pastime to beat up on our sons? But now, can you hang onto this, the faithfulness of God, even though you cannot seem to find a faithful person? Can you affirm with certain hope the presence of a faithful Father in a world that has apparently been orphaned? Can you look your situation in the teeth and shout your praise, "The Lord has saved his people"?

The Prophetic Mood

That's the mood to which the Prophet Jeremiah spoke this ancient but contemporary word. For thirty chapters in our Bible he had spoken doom, destruction, devastation, attacking the idolatry with which the land was filled, scolding them, the people of the covenant, for faithfulness and unbelief and sin against a faithful God who brought them out of Egypt, out of bondage, and had made them his own people. He likened Judah to a faithless spouse who must surely be divorced. He predicted the destruction of the temple in Jerusalem because that temple had become the nation's rabbit's foot, a good luck charm, providing the illusion of security. They had used God and his covenant for self-delusion and believed that, with the temple on Mount Zion in their midst, with the smoke of sacrifices rising to the heavens, with the temple singers doing their own thing, and with the priests still functioning in their perfunctory way, they had God's blessing on their selfish and self-centered ways. Never mind the covenant obedience.

We have to understand the prophets in their own historic situation to appreciate how their prophetic word explodes across the centuries with a dynamic word for us. Jeremiah came to the prophetic scene in Judah sometime in the latter seventh century B.C., not long before the nation would experience God's judgment through the instrument of Babylon. The Northern Kingdom, Israel, had already been destroyed a hundred years before, beneath the heel of the Assyrian, verifying prophecies of Amos and Hosea, as a judgment of the righteous God upon their spiritual adultery. Except for momentary bursts of reformation, Judah fared no better than had Israel. Their entire history, too, had been a history of ingratitude, disobedience, and faithlessness. It was Jeremiah's mission, therefore, to announce the judgment that appeared on the horizon of their limited tomorrows.

The Word of Hope

But suddenly there came this word of hope, and we recall that Jeremiah's prophecy did not include much hope. Against a background of black velvet Jeremiah placed this diamond — a facet of it here in this small paragraph of praise: "Sing aloud, raise shouts, proclaim, give praise and say, 'The Lord has saved his people.' " The day will come again!

We can read about it just a few lines forward in the chapter: "Behold, the days are coming, says the Lord, when I will make a new covenant with the house of Israel and the house of Judah." The covenant that God had made with Israel and Judah when he brought them out of Egypt had been broken, not by a faithless God, but by this faithless people. Previous prophets of the Lord, like Amos and Hosea, for example, had called for a return to faith and promised that the Lord would once again remember the covenant that he had made with them. But Jeremiah spoke in different terms. That ancient covenant was broken so completely that, in fact, there was no longer any covenant to which they could return. Their situation was so desperate that only a new covenant could serve. Their hearts had turned so far from Jahweh that obedience was not a possibility. He would give them a new heart, implant his will and law within them, and he would be their God again and they his people. He would enter on an altogether new relationship with them. "I will forgive their iniquity, and I will remember their sin no more." The relationship was founded on forgiveness.

The LORD Has Saved

Accent this, therefore: "The LORD has saved his people." "If an Ethiopian could change his skin, or if a leopard could change his spots, then perhaps a people grown accustomed to do evil could instead do good." (Jeremiah 13:12) But this could never be. By their own efforts any thought of getting their relationship with God adjusted once again was negative. To call for an obedient return could only put them on a path that leads to grief. One hope alone was still alive in Jeremiah — the hope he found in God's decision, formed in love and grace, to save. There was no other hope except the Promise of the Lord — the promise of his grace, the promise of a change of heart that God alone could give, the promise of forgiveness.

Jeremiah was not a leader in group therapy, neither a psychologist nor behavioral scientist, but he has touched the roots here of humanity's predicament — our incurably deceitful hearts. As he reflected on the bondage that refuses to give up its opposition to the Lord of heaven and earth, he concluded rightfully that it is simply not within our power to determine our own way, nor could an attempt to cleanse ourselves be more successful. Jeremiah's understanding of the human situation is the predecessor of St. Paul's lament, "O wretched man that I am," and of our own confession that "we are in bondage to sin and cannot free ourselves."

But the LORD has saved his people. The prophetic word was spoken to the exiles of the former Northern Kingdom, but the event he had in mind — salvation — was surely to be shared by all of Israel, and we claim our share, too. "The Lord has saved his people" is our own praise now, not only in the creeds we mumble or the hymns we sing, but in our breathing and our living to the praise of glory. God's new covenant, fulfilled in Christ, is in effect. His body broken on the cross, his blood poured out for us — these are the gifts of his new covenant that Christ may dwell in our hearts by faith. In the Gospel of forgiving grace he calls us not to the obedience of law, but the obedience of faith. His gracious will replaces our own stubborn wills within the heart. He has formed himself in us and molded us as his new creatures in Christ Jesus.

"Proclaim, give praise, and say, 'The Lord has saved his people.' "

If God had followed our example, as we frequently insist he ought, he would have jumped the ship a couple thousand years ago. But then there was that night in Bethlehem when God, instead of shouting, "Stop the world, I want to get off," sent angel messengers to bring the news that he had come aboard. And in response to cries of hopeless blind folk groping in the darkness of sin's night, "Jesus, son of David, save me," there was born in David's town a Savior, Christ the Lord. We know that story well and we have punctuated it with praise: "The Lord has saved his people."

Our Deepest Longing Satisfied

Here we find expressed God's answer to the deepest longing of the human heart, even though we may now know precisely what it is we long for; his answer to the deepest yearning of the world; his answer to the sorest struggle of humanity to find a way back into our lost Eden. He will gather them "from the farthest parts of the earth, among them the blind and the lame, the woman with child and her who is in travail, together; a great company, they shall return here. With weeping they shall come, and with consolations I will bring them back. I will make them walk by brooks of water, in a straight path in which they shall not stumble; for I am a father to Israel, and Ephraim is my firstborn." That's a symbol language for that whole vast company who by his saving act have been redeemed, who "from earth's wide bounds, from ocean's farthest coast, through gates of pearl stream in a countless host, singing to Father, Son, and Holy Ghost: Alleluia!" The Lord has saved his people!

Could any of us ever dream that for fulfillment of these longings we should look inside the church? We are called to preach the Gospel of his saving acts, but for all of our triumphant proclamation, is there any sign that Christ is in our midst? Do we look saved? This company of fearful, timid, unenthusiastic, listless, bored, and broken people, is there any evidence that they are going anywhere at all? One need not listen closely in our time to hear the church referred to as a has-been, or look closely to observe the desperation in the hearts of laity and clergy who are flailing in the darkness, trying to become involved in something that will justify existence. Thousands, even of her own children, have come to expect little of her in the way of salvation.

This causes me great pain, not just because I love the church and am involved in it and have not been a mere spectator in the bleachers, but because I can't forget that in this institution is the place from which the springs of life still flow. I hear the news. It tells about a world that yawns in emptiness and boredom, that is seeking something that will give life meaning. I listen to the answers and solutions of the experts, and they are dreary answers and solutions that have long ago gone bankrupt. And then I come back to the church again and the Gospel of salvation, only to discover that the springs of life are clogged with people who seem not at all the holy people of God, but for whom a holy, chosen people is the last thing that they want to be. They seem busy with their own agenda, indolent in service, indifferent in their faith and hope and love.

Yet I Believe

Yet I believe! The Gospel is a call to faith. It is an affirmation in the face of everything that seems to contradict it that "the Lord has saved his people." It needs no support or proof in giant social action programs, ecumenical alliances, or ecclesiastical displays. It needs nothing but the Promise. The seed grows secretly. The still, small voice still speaks. The Promise doesn't say that God's saved people would return like conquering heroes, but like bedraggled exiles, common folk in all the circumstances of humanity, the blind, the lame, the pregnant, with weeping and with consolations.

But the Promise stands, and it will never fail.

Proper 26 (October 30 — November 5)
Ordinary Time 31
Deuteronomy 6:1-9

Your Undivided Attention, Please

The story has been told about a beggar (I have not the faintest notion where I might have heard it) who each day took his position just outside the gate of a very rich man's house. The wealthy owner of the mansion, kind and sympathetic to the poor man's problem, but sometimes on a guilt trip over what he had and others didn't have, each day gave the beggar food and clothing and whatever else he needed to sustain his life. In return the beggar was required to do nothing.

One day the rich man had to get a message to a friend some distance from his house, and since all his servants were already busy, he wrote the message on a piece of paper, took it to the beggar, and asked him to deliver it. The beggar proudly stood up from his accustomed beggar's perch and answered, "My business, sir, is to solicit alms. I do not run errands."

The story has a double edge. Certainly the beggar was a single-minded person, faithful to the job description he had written for himself. He reminds me of the top executive whose business is to run the company, not to put on coffee for the office force. One ought not exceed the limits of one's duty. That could be a sure-footed path to burnout.

But on the other edge the fellow was an ingrate. Most wealthy folk would never tolerate their fences being decorated by a daily beggar. Much less would they supply his daily ration. He would get the word, "Begone, you devil! Get a job! This is not the welfare office!"

We Are All Beggars

Martin Luther, near his dying hour, is reported to have said, "Wir sind alle Bettler, das ist wahr." It seems more pointed and descriptive in his language than it does in ours: "We are all beggars, that is true." But what is worse, as beggars at the mansion gates of heaven, we are often reasonable facsimiles of the beggar at the rich man's gate.

Each day God gives us food and clothing, shelter and whatever else we need, the necessities of life and for a few of us a luxury or two. He surrounds us with a family of loved ones and a faithful friend or two, guards us against all danger, protects us from all evil. He assures us of his kindly disposition with a love that has delivered us from pain of sin and fear of death and threat of hell — that Egypt land where we were held in bondage until he brought us through the water of baptism into Christ. He has given us the hope of everlasting life, the promised land beyond the wilderness, shepherds whose assignment is to lead us through the wilderness, and he has given us himself. *"My presence* will go with you." He is the light who leads us on the unknown way. "I will be your God," he promises, "and you will be my people."

That's the covenant that he has made with us, the bargain he has struck with us. Bargain, certainly, for in return we are required to do nothing: nothing, that is, but to love the Lord our God, with all our hearts, with all our souls, with all our minds, with all our might. The Word and Promise that he gives shall be upon our hearts, and we shall teach it diligently to our children, speak of it at night as we retire for the day and in the morning when we rise to face another opportunity. We shall keep it between the eyes and wear it on our arms and post it on our doors.

But we respond, "My business, sir, is to solicit alms. I do not run errands." "My job description, sir, is to receive your blessings, not to do a blessed thing beyond that."

The Word today imposes that impossible demand: "You shall love the Lord your God with all your heart and soul and mind and strength, and you shall love your neighbor as yourself." To recognize this as the claim of God upon our lives is better than all whole burnt offerings and sacrifices, and he who recognizes this is not far from the kingdom. But in a world of sorry neighbors and where we are often sorry neighbors, too, and in a life from which God often seems so desperately distant, this undivided love for God and neighbor is beyond attainment.

Hear, O Israel

Your undivided attention, please! The word today is in the Book of Deuteronomy, the word of Moses to the people Israel whom he had led for forty years across the wilderness from Egypt. This is his final exhortation and encouragement before they were to cross the Jordan to the Promised Land of Canaan. They had been beggars through those years, totally depended on the goodness of the Lord, but for the most part disobedient, ungrateful, and complaining beggars. The land of Canaan lay ahead of them. The promise of that land was soon to be fulfilled.

But it would not be easy over there. There would still be much to challenge faith and quicken fear and threaten trust and tempt to disobedience. As they mixed it up with Canaanites, especially with their false gods and cultic rites, they would experience a constant threat to faithlessness. Therefore, the Word:

Hear, O Israel: The Lord our God is one Lord; and you shall love the Lord your God with all your heart, and with all your soul, and with all your might. And these words which I command you this day shall be upon your heart; and you shall teach them diligently to your children, and shall talk to them when you sit in your house, and when you walk by the way, and when you lie down, and when you rise.

Hear, O Israel! Give me your undivided attention, please!

Gratitude in Action

That's the message of the Book of Deuteronomy, a series of appeals for gratitude in action. And that's the word today. You are a people set apart and holy. You are the beneficiaries of all his saving acts on your behalf. You are the people brought together by his grace, called from bondage into freedom, called from darkness into light, called from living death to deathless life. Remember that! Stick it in your ear and don't forget it. Fasten it between your eyes and don't lose sight of it. Love the Lord your God. Cling to him alone as he has clung in faithful love to you. Your undivided attention, please!

And now in passing, although not so much in passing, but to make a point, there are two new words for our vocabulary that this paragraph suggests. "Hear, O Israel, the Lord our God is one Lord!" Your attention, please! Known as the Shema, taken from the first word of the sentence in the Hebrew — *hear* — this became Judaism's confession of faith. This line became the spiritual battle cry of Israel and still remains so to this day. Hear! Stick it in your ear! And from this paragraph as well the practice of phylacteries developed, those small receptacles of cube-shaped leather worn by male Jews on their foreheads and their arms at prayer times. "Bind them as a sign upon your hand, and they shall be as frontlets between your eyes." And down the years to Jesus Christ, when a scribe heard him disputing with the Sadducees and delicately asked the question, "Which commandment is the first of all?" Jesus answered with the unassailable Shema, "The first is this, 'Hear, O Israel: The Lord, our God, the Lord is one . . . ' "

Pure Grace

The word in Deuteronomy does not in any sense imply that Israel could earn salvation by obedience. It is simply and directly a call for their undivided attention, to love the Lord and cling to him alone as their response to love that God had shown to them. All the saving acts of God had been on their behalf, and they were acts of grace, and Israel's relationship with God had been established in no lesser way than by the grace of God. But given grace, their job description was spelled out. You are a people holy to the Lord, set apart, consecrated! Love the Lord your God! Undivided attention! No more, no less!

Marked With the Cross

Tell me, now. Do you recognize the word, the promise, the voice? "You are a people holy to the Lord." Do you remember how you got that way? On your forehead, right between the eyes, you have been marked with the cross of Christ forever. The Holy Spirit of the living one true God has stuck it in your ear, the Gospel of God's saving act at Calvary where he broke in on death's dominion and delivered us from every claim that hell could make on us. We have been given a new life. We are the heirs of every blessing flowing from his hand. Is there anything that we have earned, that we have not received in grace?

There is always the anxiety in Deuteronomy lest Israel might forfeit her salvation, struggle free from Jahweh's claim of grace on her, divide attention due to him alone with other gods or with themselves. The anxiety may also be our own. There are temptations on our way. Divided hearts, indifferent praise, self-centered service, the false gods of America that peer seductively from every bush, all these are dangers on the way. We know the traps, and how often our feet, too, are caught in them. And worst of all, that first and basic sin when we enthrone ourselves as center of the empire and surround ourselves like little kings with all the alms we have solicited from God to serve our comforts and our needs and our insatiable appetite for things — that propensity is also ours. "My business, sir, is to solicit alms. I do not run errands."

Hear, O Israel: Your attention, please: The Lord our God, the Lord is one. Stick it in your ear and paste it on your forehead, but the change is in your heart, for you shall love the Lord your God with undivided fervor . . . and you shall love your neighbor as yourself.

And every day there will be errands we can run.

Proper 27 (November 6-12)
Ordinary Time 32
1 Kings 17:8-16

Home Economy

This style of home economy is difficult to find today. In fact, the story that God spreads before us as our diet for this harvest Sunday is so far removed from the complexities of poverty in our society, the issues of world hunger, and the problems of production that it seems a legend, something out of this world. Things like this don't happen any more. We would hardly want to teach this style of home economy in our home economics classes.

Much to our regret and loss, God seems to have been sent off into space aboard Columbia and left to float there. It would be useless to concern him with our small concerns — those questions that keep popping from our lips like, "What's to eat? And what's to drink?" What would he know about it anyway? The God of Sunday morning is the God who tells us in the Apostolic Word to "live in the Spirit!" What good is he across the week when we are constantly reminded by the denture cream commercials and by the pressures on the billfold that we live in the flesh?

Who is in Control?

But the move to lift God into seventh heaven while we assume control of earthly problems never works. There is no reason to believe that our control has been effective. This fantastic story happened. This style of home economy, so difficult to find among wastemakers of America, this happened. It happened at a place called Zarapheth, just a stone's throw inland from the sea coast and thirty miles from the unheard-of city of Beirut. It happened at a time in history when Ahab ruled in Israel and when his fair wife, Jezebel, had managed to effect an intimate acquaintance for her husband with the false god Baal. It concerns the food supply, and hunger, and whatever else we need for the support of life and limb. It happened not as a result of an ingenious program planned by Ahab's agriculture secretary, but as God's provision. God gave his word, and with his word a minimum daily income, and whether we are always with it on that score, we have depended on that kind of action ever since with the simple vital prayer, "Give us this day our daily bread."

No one questions the necessity of sharing with the hungry of the world or working at the problems of ecology, war, overpopulation, waste. Our concern for one another in the human family can never rest while there are starving millions, undernourished children, eyes sunken in their sockets in despair. But *the first lesson* in this text is this: home economy begins with this dimension (for which so many of us have advanced glaucoma), that "the eyes of all wait upon thee, O Lord."

I don't know what Ahab thought of his administration as the king of Israel, or how he would have had historians describe it. There have been kings and presidents who have been more concerned with history's view of them than they have been concerned with loving mercy, doing justly, and walking humbly with their God. But God's view of Ahab has to be a little different from Ahab's own, for the record has it that King Ahab did evil in the sight of the Lord more than all that were before him. For twenty-two long years, his administration spelled disaster. He dethroned the God of Israel in favor of Baal, exiled Jahweh for a god more groovy.

But if the God who in the poetry of Gerhardt "points the clouds their courses, whom winds and waves obey" is exiled, and if the God who makes the rain and dew and sets the chemistry of soil in motion to produce the crops is banished, then there will be no rain or dew.

The Drought

So there was drought. For three long years the land was parched, and if we remember Minnesota in three weeks of rainless skies, maybe we can understand what happens in three years. There were no crops, the soil cracked and turned to dust, the streams dried up, and famine gripped the people — thirst, starvation, hunger, malnutrition — all words familiar in the social circumstances of the 1980s.

But then, as now, not everybody suffered. There were those who had the knack of being able to convert the circumstances to their own benefit, who profited in blight. Injustices became the order of the day. Oppression was the rule of thumb, and everybody in the struggle tried to step on everybody else to get what they could get, even if it meant the deprivation of another.

In the town of Zarapheth there lived a widow with her only son, and to preserve Elijah in the famine, God sent him to her. "She will feed you," God said in what would have to be the impossible promise. But Elijah, unlike most of us, accustomed to believe the word and promise of his God, went to Zarapheth, only to discover that the widow had no loaded pantry, no humus, no falafel, no tabbouleh, nor even a dried piece of kaffee kuchen. She was on her final ration — a handful of meal in the jar and a little oil in the cruse, and she was gathering sticks with which to build a fire so that her boy and she could eat once more before they died.

"Go, do as I have asked," Elijah said. "First, bake a loaf of bread for me, and then when I am taken care of, you will have one for yourself."

And how about that? A Prophet of the Lord insisting that he have first bat, as selfish as all that. Social insensitivity? Did he not realize that there was famine in the land, that he was doing this poor widow in?

The Promise

Go for it, Elijah must have thought, for God has promised. And he acted on the promise. He had just come from the brook Cherith where the Lord had sent the ravens with his bread and meat each morning and more bread and meat each evening. And in that period of intensive, special care, he never worried what would happen if the brook dried up. He lived in faith, the faith that if God feeds the birds on wing and clothes the lilies of the field, will he not take care of us as well?

We can use a little of that trust and confidence — that inspired boldness, holy recklessness, and fearless faith — faith that casts out fear because it isn't faith in our capacity to play the role of God and keep our little empires from collapse, but faith that rests on him. We are not without experience in seeing how God keeps his word. Do we say that these things never happen anymore? They happen every day, not by the mighty hand of man, but by the hand of God.

The widow also took God at his word. She did as Elijah ordered, and they ate for many days. The jar of meal was never spent, neither did the cruse of oil fail. Home economy to make the home economist take notice! Provision to amaze the farmers of the western plains!

Something to Learn

God dynamites some lessons from this incident that should explode in our faces and within our hearts. One of them is this, that he as our Creator God is still the God of his Creation. Whatever errors we might find in distribution of creation's goods are ours, not his. And this is Gospel, too, to say as plainly and as simply as our cluttered minds can stand, that God's provisions are abundant, that God has stocked the larder, that God supplies enough for all whose habitation this world is. He is the God of love whose extravagance is overwhelming.

But our response to his extravagance is not extravagance, but stewardship; not waste, but care — the most intensive care we can accord to his resources. For our natural resources are not natural. They are miracles. Air pollution is a problem of concern, not because God hasn't given us the air to breathe, and not that we must be concerned with his supply, but because of what we do with it to spoil it as the plastic world makes plastic profits with its plastic products. The junk yards and the garbage pits are our concern — not because God piled them there, but because we fail him in our stewardship. Food distribution is a problem, not because God has gone bankrupt, but because we have.

For *the second lesson* that explodes in front of us at Zarapheth is this: that we have a distribution problem. It's a matter of our use, of knowing where provisions come from, what their purpose is, for whom they are intended, and what to do with them. The widow knew — knew that our Father feeds us and that he feeds others through us, and that even when the food supply has been exhausted, our Father feeds us still, and we can go from where we are through death itself to know that his good will has never failed. When I have banished that old outdated thought, of course, then I am in trouble. Or when I plainly wish to do no more than hand out doles to beggars so that my compassion is admired, then I am in trouble. When I want to look like God and be sure that others recognize me in that role, when I snap judgments on the lazy poor or on the filthy rich, then I am in trouble.

First This

But when I know where these provisions come from, that their source is our Creator and our Father and the Giver God who opens hands so lavishly, and when I know that he does not intend them for a few of us but all of us; and when I add on top of that what he has done in Jesus Christ for me to be assured that it is really he who lavishes his love like this —

• then I will see my fellows not as beggars but as brothers, sisters, and as children with me in the human family,

• not as people to be helped from my exalted throne, but as persons who share my predicament as beggar under God,

• not as people whom I can enslave to serve my profit, but as hearts with whom my own can be entangled.

Life's program, then, is not a grabby, but a gracious thing.

And *lesson three* is this: your heavenly Father knows that you have need. He knows also what we need to change our hearts, to get that new perspective of ourselves as those who have been made his children in the death of Christ, a new perspective on our sisters in the human family, and new perspective of our role. When we take God at his word and promise, that word and promise dictate a new course of life. And on the course we will encounter one surprise upon another. Let this word be the starter's gun: "Seek first his kingdom and his righteousness (that's faith, dependence, trust), and all these things shall be yours as well."

Proper 28 (November 13-19)
Ordinary Time 33
Daniel 7:9-14

What Was That About?

Our first reaction to the reading of a paragraph like this one from the Book of Daniel is to shake loose from the long, blank stare of disbelief and ask, "Just what was *that* about?"

If we heard aright, it seemed to paint the picture of an old man sitting on a throne of fiery flame, surrounded by ten thousand times ten thousand equally strange looking creatures, and it seemed to say that this was something like a courtroom where the record books were open and a judgment soon to be pronounced. Suddenly great clouds appear, and in the clouds one like a son of man who stands before the Ancient One. And the son of man receives the kingdom and the power and the glory — a kingdom that shall never pass away and one that cannot be destroyed. All people, languages, and nations bow before him.

The Word today, just what is this about? Our curiosity is stimulated. If this is right (and our suspicions are confirmed that we will hear about the Judgment Day), does anybody take that seriously?

If there are quarters where that mentality persists and where the possibility of final judgment is at least acknowledged, why bring that up? It seems to me we have some judgments to contend with now, and these are quite enough without becoming exercised about a judgment on some distant day. Self-styled judges are in great supply. Don't tell me there's another waiting in the wings to nail me at the end of history.

In particular, what shall we say to this — this ancient vision of a psychopathic character named Daniel who admits it in these very words,

Daniel had a dream and visions in his head as he lay in his bed.

Apocalyptic

Just what is this about? Before we go too far, let me explain that the Book of Daniel is apocalyptic, which is to say that like the Revelation of St. John, which closes the New Testament, the Book of Daniel is a writing that was born in circumstances of the most severe historic crisis, yet looked beyond the crisis to the final victory of God. Apocalyptic literature spoke of current events of its own time in language that was largely imagery and symbol, a fact that poses difficulty in precise identification of the characters involved. It looked forward to a time when God would intervene in history to bring an end to evil and establish good.

But if we ask, "What is this all about?" we can affirm that in its time this is about the empire of the Babylonians, its successor powers in the Medes and Persians, and the empire of the Greeks. But the Word is never static. If we grab it by the beard and drag it through the years and lay it on the line marked 1985 (or 1988 . . . or 1991 . . .), this speaks to us about a world of nations as we know them now — (Name them!). We can throw in other names if we would like — Nebuchadnezzar, King Darius, Antiochus Epiphanes — or names of high and mighty in our own time, too, but in particular, the name of him who was around before we got here, is in our midst today, and will be here long after we are gone — Jesus Christ, the Alpha and Omega, the Beginning and the End, the First and Last. This paragraph portrays participants in the parade of nations — kingdoms on the rise and kingdoms on the wane — and finally the kingdom and the power, the dominion and the glory that is everlasting. This underscores the power and stability of faith available to us for such a time as this.

Strong Faith

The intention of the writer, here called Daniel, was to describe God's purpose in the history of the world and to encourage all the saints to faith that cannot be perturbed by crises, persecutions, or what seems to be defeat. The Book of Daniel is the product of its history. It was born in the religious, the political, the economic circumstances of the times, and it expresses both the hopes and fears that echo and re-echo the faith of God's own people. It was designed to strengthen faith, encourage hope, and — at a time when all seemed hopeless, as it does for multitudes today — to vindicate that faith and hope.

Although the scene is set in Babylon during the captivity, the book was written to address a period of persecution under King Antiochus Epiphanes, about 164 BC. Just before this paragraph, Daniel tells us that he saw four beasts — a winged lion and a bear, a four-headed leopard, and finally a fourth beast, terrible and dreadful and exceedingly strong, with ten horns, and different from the beasts that went before it.

With this imagery and symbol, Daniel has described four nations — Babylon, the Medes, the Persians, and finally the Greeks — the beast whose ten horns represent the ten kings following Alexander and who finally gave way to still another horn — Antiochus Epiphanes. It was this last-named ruler who was determined at whatever cost to wipe out every trace of Jewish faith. He banned the practice of the faith with all its rites and ceremonies. He built an altar to the Greek god Zeus within the temple court. He oppressed them, persecuted them, and finally obliterated as many of them who would not adopt the culture of the Greek.

In the midst of this came this prophetic word to strengthen faith, encourage hope. The issue was not one of politics or economics. This was a spiritual struggle for the faith. So the images are painted in sharp contrast — light vs. darkness, good vs. evil, God vs. Satan. And God's chosen people are portrayed against the background of the nations where the powers of wickedness had been entrenched. Our extremities are God's opportunities. The time is short. The end God has appointed certainly is near. Hang tough. Keep the faith. This is their hour and the power of darkness.

But as I looked, "thrones were placed and one that was Ancient of Days took his seat . . . thousand thousands served him and ten thousand times ten thousand stood before him . . . and behold with the clouds of heaven there came one like a son of man, and he came to the Ancient of Days and was presented before him . . . and to him was given dominion and glory and kingdom." Doesn't this sound strangely similar to Jesus' word recorded by St. Mark?

*"And then they will see the Son of Man coming in clouds
with great power and glory. And then he will send out the
angels and gather his elect from the four winds, from the
ends of the earth to the ends of heaven."*

Great Hope

And what's that all about? If I lost you somewhere in the woods
of all this history, you can find your way out here. This is about
great hope. This is about the Christian in a threatening world
today, who, because he holds an insane hope for a returning Lord,
who shouts in faith that God is Lord of history and that the final
victory belongs to him, can live in these dark days of momentary
setbacks, knowing they are only momentary.

At a time when atheism seems to triumph, when materialism
rules, when even in the church the devil seems to have the upper
hand and the Christian witness is completely negative — judgment,
vengeance, personal profit seeking — the child of God can remain
unperturbed. He can look back on the mad convulsions of our age
that spell disaster even for the cause of God and be surprised to see
that even now, amid the surging chaos of these times, God is at
work to build his kingdom in a way that, although hidden at this
point, will one day be revealed. It's a bit like Jesus sleeping in the
ship tossed on the billows of the stormy water. "Be not afraid."

Now you can read with your tongue in cheek opinionated
columnists who map the future.

If you are young and see the future as a threat, you can stand on
this great hope and see an altogether different life ahead for you.

If you are older and the sunset years are rushing in, you can
know that life is open-ended.

If you are bruised and buffeted and beaten, you know in this
faith that your chin need not drag on your chest continually.

And if you shake your head at headlines, and if you ask, "What
is this world coming to?" that isn't difficult to answer. We know
what this world's coming to. The past, the present, and the future
— all are in the hands of God. His purposes will ripen fast.

Enthusiastic Joy

This is the faith we hold, and the reason for the hope that is in us, and why we might expect a more enthusiastic joy reflected in our lives. God has already given us a guarantee. He has brought us out of death to life in Jesus Christ. He has given us down payment with the gift of his life-giving Spirit. The covenant of purchase has been sealed, and he who spared not his own Son, but freely gave him for us all, will he not give us all things with him? We may still be engaged in battle, but the war has been won. In our own lives, too, the powers of evil can so easily become entrenched and gain the momentary victory. We show the battle scars, and frequently the bleeding wounds of sin, and often, too, the wounds and scars inflicted by the sin and guilt of others. God still has some work to do on us — especially on you and me, it's obvious — but he has given us the promise, and we look forward to that day of victory when God is everything, when nothing stands between us.

Now

In the hope of God's fulfillment, the victory of the Son of Man, the certainty of the kingdom and the power and the glory, we can also enjoy the miracle of now. That "Now Generation" that we used to hear about is gone, but we are NOW. The burden of the past is lifted; the future is assured. It's NOW. As one great preacher of the century has said it, "We may not know *what* is coming, but we do know *who* is coming."

So we can live.

Christ the King
Jeremiah 23:2-6

And He Shall Reign

Just one more word we need to say and one more thing we need to do on this last Sunday of another year with Christ. We said it last year and the year before, and we will say it next year and the year beyond, and we will say it when the morning of his glory dawns and every knee will bend with us before his throne: *Christ is King! He shall reign forever!*

While the Ronald Reagans and the Walter Mondales and the Yuri Andropovs and the Fidel Castros and the Yassar Arafats flash momentarily like meteorites across the skies of history . . .

While the nations conspire and the people plot in vain, and the kings of the earth set themselves, and the rulers take counsel together against the Lord and against his Anointed . . . He who sits in the heavens laughs.

"I have set my king on Zion, my holy hill . . . You are my Son, today I have begotten you. Ask of me, and I will make the nations your heritage, and the ends of the earth your possessions."

The Lord reigns, he is throned in majesty; the Lord is robed, he is girded with strength. The world is established; it shall never be moved; thou art from everlasting.

. . . These are the trumpets heralding the coming of the King. This is the language of the coronation!

Our Many-Splendored Lord

Sometimes in this past year, while walking with the Lord (I trust you did), we claimed him as our Savior. And it's well we did, because we need a Savior who is able to bring good news in the midst of all our bad news, release from sin with its oppressive guilt and strangling power, deliverance from the ruts of evil habit we have grooved . . .

Sometimes when the pain became unbearable and there was nothing in the pill box or the liquor cabinet that helped, we claimed him as the Good Physician, someone who could heal our self-inflicted wounds, relieve the pain and soften hurts that we have brought upon ourselves or others. It's well we did because, for all our progress, medicine still has one death for every customer . . .

Sometimes we took his hand and called him Gentle Shepherd, for in a world of noisy violence we need gentility at times, and someone who can find the greener pastures that we couldn't find ourselves and protect us from the bramble bushes on the way. Going our way hasn't been as liberating as we thought it might be . . .

Sometimes we claimed him as a stronger Brother, someone we could trust and lean on when a fellow needs a friend, especially in a day when friends who can be trusted are so rare . . .

But today we make no claims on Christ. We only need at last to recognize his claim on us.

We ask nothing for ourselves. The tables turn and he asks everything from us. He who came to serve the sinner in great meekness, as an old hymn has it, now claims us to serve him with our lives.

That means that he lays claim to every moment on the time clock, every penny in our pockets, every heartbeat in our chest.

Christ is King! The Lord reigns! He through whom all things were made, for whom all things exist, in whom all things are glued together, he is robed in majesty. And he shall reign!

Then why are we unglued and nervous, off-the-wall and anxious (or however one describes the jitters of the jokers who pretend to run our world).?

The Prophet Speaks

The Word today is good news on the lips of Jeremiah, a Word

of hope when everything is hopeless, even "The Day After." We should note that in his word this prophet had no comment on the Lord as Good Physician, nor as a Gentle Shepherd as the lead theme of a pastorale, nor even as a Savior. The people he addressed denied God's claim on them and went their own way, belied the covenant that God had made with them, sold out to belly interests that they thought more satisfying, and expected God to bless them for it.

How often, like the spiral of a cycle, history is repeated. The nightly news in those days was as bleak and dismal as the nightly news in ours.

But Jeremiah doesn't want us to forget it. The Lord reigns! And behold the days are coming, and there will be some changes made.

I grant you that it doesn't look that way, and perhaps we ought to be the more alert to human folly when it does, when everything is going our way and the future seems to dawn with promise on the lives that we have taken into our own hands. You heard the Prophet, didn't you — or did you? Frequently what people hear is not exactly what was said. He spoke of shepherds who mislead the flock and scatter them. His targets were the kings of Judah and their nobles, "shepherds" as he called them, the political and military leaders who had brought the flock of God to exile and defeat, disgrace and devastation. They had inherited the promises of God, the covenant that God had made with David, of a throne that would endure forever. And while they basked within its warmth, they had failed in its responsibility. They had fleeced the sheep and scattered them, led their people into faithlessness, idolatry, injustices, and immorality of every kind. The final end could only be their judgment under God in the worst humiliation the land had ever known.

Lessons from History

There is history here that we should know about, for not to know it is to live it through again, and we are dangerously close to that. It is not the kind of history that one hears about in Sunday School, as familiar as eye-popping stories of the heroes, Joseph, Moses, Daniel. Jeremiah doesn't get much ink in children's literature, except as a frustrated prophet. His word was for the most part doom, and its fulfillment gruesome in its most minute detail.

As the nation Judah neared its end about 600 years before our Lord, three kings in rapid order (or *dis*order , if you will) ruled Judah on the throne of David: Jehoiakim, Johoiakin, and Zedekiah. The last one, Zedekiah (whose name, significantly, meant "The Lord our Righteousness") was nothing but a weakling left behind to rule this decimated people and their devastation after all the cream of Judah's leadership had been deported into Babylon. But there were still a few whose hopes rode high on Zedekiah, who expected miracles from God that would upset the Babylonian, restore their nation, and permit them to get on with life as usual. So they staged continuing rebellion against Babylon with no result except that Babylon returned to spray Jerusalem again and finish off the place completely. Jeremiah had predicted that — that there would be no miracles; that God, in fact, was on the side of Babylon against this faithless people who were rotten to the core. Judah as it had been known would be no more.

Attention!

But your attention, please! The crisis was more than political. It was theological. The nation's misplaced faith and false security had been swept out from under it, and, hanging in the thin air of disaster, it had collapsed completely.

This "flock of God" had had the covenant of God with Abraham ("We are children of Abraham"). They had had the covenant of God with Moses ("I will be your God, and you will be my people"). They had had the covenant of God with David — that of his throne, established forever, there would be no end. And there on Zion was the seat of God, the Holy Temple, the rabbit's foot that sealed his promises, assured prosperity regardless of behavior.

But all these misplaced hopes were shattered now. Jerusalem had crumbled, the Temple lay in ruins, the Ark of the Covenant was nothing but charred wood, and the people were forced to live in a strange land. They had forgotten that holiness befits the Lord's house, and they were under judgment. The nightly news reported Judah's devastation. The prophetic word reported it as judgment brought upon themselves for faithlessness. The crisis: Had God failed? Had he broken covenant with them? Or was the god of Babylon a more successful god than Jahweh?

Hope!

But while the Prophet had no hope for Judah in its faithlessness and disobedience, he was not altogether hopeless. The people had been faithless. God was not. They were under judgment. God could never be.

> *Behold, the days are coming, says the Lord, when I will raise up for David a righteous Branch, and he shall reign as king and deal wisely, and shall execute justice and righteousness in the land. In his days Judah shall be saved, and Israel will dwell securely. And this is the name by which he shall be called: "The Lord is our righteousness!"*

This is the certainty of faith that Jeremiah coveted for Judah and so desperately sought to share with them. This is the certainty he shares with us when life seems at its darkest hour and the promises of God seem little more than pious rhetoric and we hang in the thin air of our own disasters, waiting for the final blow to strike. God is faithful. His promise will be vindicated. There will be a faithful residue whom God will gather in from all the nations where they had been driven . . . and the throne of David, as the covenant has said, would be continued in that righteous Branch who would be called "The Lord our justice."

Now we can overlay on Jeremiah's word of hope the good news of Christ, the righteous Branch. This prophetic legacy our Lord could not forget. He came to heal the sick, to gather up the lost sheep of the House of Israel, to implant a new heart in the breasts of people, and to rule in righteousness and justice. The royal trappings were conspicuous by absence. The manger was his castle, the cross his throne, his conquering army that sad looking lot of fisher folk and erstwhile tax collectors. He rose from the ranks of a carpenter's son in the alleys of Nazareth — to bring good news for the poor, liberty for the oppressed, sight for the blind, and release for the captives. And when he died, the victim of his own compassion, the sacrifice of his own justice, and the exemplar of his own righteousness, he left behind him nothing but redemption, the forgiveness of sins, and peace through the blood of his cross.

That's how he lays his righteousness on us, stamps his claim of love on us, and grants a whole new vision of what life is all about.

He doesn't promise blessings on our schemes for self-advancement, or a winking eye at our unrighteous dealings with our fellows in exchange for pious moments here and there. He will not be used as good luck charms we carry in our pockets. He claims us as his own — his subjects and his servants who, in the obedience and quiet confidence of faith, live lives that crown him Lord of all.